Table of Conte

HELL IN PARADISE

Foreword

Our prosperity as a nation depends on our people, our ability to foresee the future and to select the right leaders to guide us in the proper direction. That is the vehicle that will determine our destination.

Hell in Paradise is about Jamaica; a small beautiful island in the Caribbean, with dirty politics and uncaring leaders. I will illustrate how the elected leaders have failed the country and have allowed it to become one of the poorest countries in the world and one with close to the highest murder rate. I will show how corruption is rewarded, while the people who play by the rules are punished. Despite the fact that the country is rich in natural resources, the vast majority of people are poor and many live on the rough edges of life.

The descendants of the slave owners still remain in control and our colonial legacy still guides our system of government and our educational doctrine remains in the firm control of the British relic.

The Jamaican people are proud and resourceful. The country has produced many mega stars in music and sports. The resilience of the people sometimes forces them to distant places searching for a better life. They leave an indelible mark wherever they go.

The main aim of this book is for it to be widely read and hopefully every Jamaican, or anyone who has heard of Jamaica, or is interested in visiting; will get a hold of a copy. They will be fascinated with a brief look at our history and some remarkable accomplishments. We have had some rough patches and in this book we will offer some practical solutions to change that situation.

Hell in Paradise: The Underbelly of Jamaican Politics

Bill Clarke, one of Jamaica's most popular bankers, was fired from his job from the Bank Of Nova Scotia Jamaica Limited- the largest bank in Jamaica. He gave a speech recently proclaiming Jamaica a failed State. That speech, along with other instances in which he came out against the status quo placed him into the doghouse with the elite in the society. This is how the Jamaican society operates. In spite of the false claim that it has a robust democracy and a legacy of freedom of speech; you will be sidelined if you express views that seemingly go against standard practices. As a loud mouth you will be made to shut up.

This book is not about Bill Clarke but will show how the Jamaican society has been stifled by the politicians and the upper class. Many of them are white and some are of a lighter complexion who have oppressed the largely ninety five percent dark-skinned people. Many of these people have been made to live in ghettos, slums and political garrisons where either of the two main political parties control and dominate communities. These areas over the years have been forced to vote for either the Peoples National Party or the Jamaica Labor Party or have had people loyal to the party migrate to that community. With the aim of showing massive majorities in elections, in many instances, over-voting with over one hundred percent of the voters listed voting for the desired politician.

Jamaica is a very beautiful country measuring about 4,411 square miles and is located about ninety miles from Cuba. It is considered as one of the most beautiful places on earth by many people who have had the great pleasure of visiting this beautiful tropical isle.

The country was like America. First inhabited by Indians, then captured by Christopher Columbus in the name of the Spanish Monarchy and was later stolen by the British, who quickly used the island as a plantation for its sugar production. This labor-intensive crop needed strong people to maintain the plantations and the British went to West Africa to capture slaves to take them back to the Caribbean. They were brought here in the most horrible conditions but they have survived and have left a rich legacy of proud black descendants. The British have also left us with their system of government, which has been bastardized by our politicians. By and large, they seek power to maintain the status quo and to advance improvements for their immediate families and close friends.

Despite being so small, the country has produced great people in music; such as Shaggy, Sean Paul, Jimmy Cliff, and Bob Marley. Bob Marley is world renowned and the champion against oppression. He used his music to educate the masses and to inspire millions around the globe. He echoed the words of his fellow countryman Marcus Garvey, to emancipate ourselves from mental slavery. Garvey had earlier in the century brought enlightenment to the blacks to the United States via his United Negro Improvement Association (UNIA).

This small beautiful island has produced some of the greatest track athletes in the world. Herb McKenly, Donald Quarrie, Merlene Ottey and more recently, the World and Olympic champion of the 100 and 200 meters, the magnificent and electrifying Usain Bolt. Many people the world overare amazed at our athletes' prowess and wonder. What is in our DNA or our diet that allows us to produce the greatest sprinters per capita on the entire planet?

Shawn Johnson

Hell in Paradise:

The Underbelly of Jamaican Politics

AUTHOR

HELL IN PARADISE

Published in the United States
by Roses Publishing Inc., Florida

Hell in Paradise/Shawn Johnson
ISBN 978-0-615-38891-5

This book is dedicated to the resilient Jamaican people

Our people are blessed with a warm spirit and magnetic personalities. This has attracted many people to the island. Many professionals have visited and refused to return to their homelands. Millions of tourists visit our beaches and all-inclusive hotels, our ital trails in Negril and wonderful South Coast charm. Unfortunately our capital city of Kingston, which is the cultural Mecca, has not been able to attract many visitors due to the crime and violence. There is squalor and run-down infrastructure, especially in the garrison communities mentioned earlier. Rural folks are afraid to venture into Kingston. The people in Kingston are nonetheless happy and cheerful and carry a smile on their faces most of the times. It seems that they have become immune to the crime and grime which has engulfed them. There is a great deal of fear but life still goes on. Many areas are like ghost towns as soon as night falls.

Jamaica in the last ten years 2000-2009 has had over fifteen thousand of its people murdered. Many of these murders go undetected and leave the murderers to go commit more murders. Other violent crimes are a common feature of the landscape; machete wounding, knife slashing, stone throwing and other kinds of violence dominate the very limited resources of the inland's hospitals.

A walk around the city will reveal the high level of unemployment among the young people. Young men gather on the street corners and are either involved in playing dominoes, card games, a soccer game of scrimmage, or they are on the look-out for a defenseless prey, which they may rob or kill. The card games and dominoes are usually played for money in a form of illegal gambling that is common across the country. While gambling or hanging out, the young men are usually charged up with multiple use of smoking the highest grade of marijuana, which they call 'spliff'. This is meticulously rolled like a cigar and the saliva used to cement the ends of the Rizla, which is the favored paper with the marijuana. On many occasions a

Chillum Pipe, that is an instrument that is filled with marijuana also known as ganja, is lit and passed around in a circle and each person huffs and puffs from a plastic pipe and gives off a huge ball of smoke.

A new phenomenon is the mixture of marijuana and cocaine mixed together. It is giving the young people an unprecedented 'high' and is also reflected in the nature of the violent crimes.

These ghettos and their link with politics, with the Jamaica Labour Party (JLP) on the one hand and the People's National Party (PNP) on the other, has turned many of these youths on the corners into community enforcers. The likes of which have produced notorious figures such as Burry Boy, Copper, Claudius Massop, Jim Brown, Tony Brown, Satta John, Natty Morgan, Sandokhan and Bulbie. Many of these people had direct link to the politicians at the highest levels and were considered untouchables by members of the security forces. The police had to turn a blind eye to their nefarious activities, in order to avoid being transferred to some rural areas. That is usually initiated by the politicians and carried out by a superior officer. The politicians dictated what happened inside the police force and that deepened the high levels of corruption.

Many of these gunslingers who worked for the politicians would sometimes think that they were more powerful than their bosses and that would signal that their reign would soon come to an end. They are usually killed by their cronies or by the police in alleged shootouts and it is usually suspected that they were ordered dead by some higher-up.

The more contemporary gun-slingers are not as controlled by the politicians as those earlier enforcers. They had the opportunity of hindsight and realized that their predecessors were used by the politicians and then dispensed with. They also realized that the politicians no longer had the Cold War dollars and that they had to seek alternatives. They moved aggressively into the drug trade and illegal gun trade and this provided a stable and sometimes ostentatious lifestyle that fit their personalities.

Much of the income garnered by these dons during the 70's and 80's was provided directly by 'cold war' foes, the United States and the Soviet Union. Jamaica was not left out of this nuclear era power struggle. The PNP represented and was supported by the Soviets, while the Americans were in the corner of the JLP. Money was awash to support these garrison communities and the effect twenty to thirty years later has proven to be devastating for these communities.

The crime statistics today illustrates the irrational and criminal decisions taken by the politicians to divide the people into two warring camps. The areas that are now known as garrisons produce seventy-two percent of the crimes in the country and eighty percent of the murders. Many of these crimes are committed using the gun. The gun gave them a sense of invincibility and power over other members of the community and as a result they controlled a great deal of the resources that came through the area.

These more recent criminals have moved into the drug trade and with the latest technologies available to them, they have been cashing in handsomely and they have used their firepower to stave off poachers. The drug trade has now become a post-slavery 'triangular trade'. The Colombians take guns and cocaine to Jamaica, then the Jamaicans facilitate the export of the drugs to the United States and then, the money is sent back to Colombia. Recently, Haiti has been playing a major role in illegal gun distribution and

has flooded the Jamaican market with this commodity. This is vitally needed in the ghettos for turf protection and the continued drug running. The sale and rental of illegal guns has become very big business in Jamaica. There are reports that the rental of guns are priced according to their size and a M16 rifle can fetch up to forty thousand dollars a day on short term rental.

1960's

In the 1960's Jamaica embarked upon a process of industrialization under a guy named Robert 'Bob' Lightbourne. He brought many industries to the country to manufacture their goods here. Common among those entities were Colgate, Gillette, Rayton Manufacturing, and other notable giants of industry. He also stimulated and inspired local industries to produce, of which Serv-Wel will be remembered. The country experienced unprecedented growth under Lightbourne's leadership of the Ministry of Industry and Commerce. The bauxite industry also took on new legs during this period. So popular was Jamaica's industrialization that the Singaporean government sent its civil servants to Jamaica to study its Industrial Policy. Forty years later Singapore is a First World country with one of the highest per capita incomes in the world, while Jamaica's manufacturing base has been completely eroded and is still considered a Third World country. It has very low per capita income and is one of the most indebted countries in the entire universe.

During Lightbourne's years, the economy grew at a rate of between six and eight percent per annum. That growth however, did not translate into too much improvement into the lives of the ordinary Jamaican people and that made them disaffected with the political process.

The late 60's brought about a new sense of social awakening, with the oppressed fighting for their rights. From the streets of Montgomery, Alabama with Dr Martin Luther King to suburban homes of disenfranchised women, unable to vote, to the slums of Kingston, Jamaica, where Walter Rodney was declared persona no grata by the Jamaican government of the day for articulating for the social improvement of the masses.

According to Wikipedia Rodney was born to a working class family in Guyana, he was a bright student, attending Queen's College in Guyana and then attending university on a scholarship at the University of the West Indies in Jamaica, graduating in 1963.

Rodney earned his PhD in 1966 at the School of Oriental and African Studies in London, England. His dissertation focused on the slave trade on the upper Guinea coast. The thesis was published in 1970 under the title A History of the Upper Guinea Coast, 1545-1800 and it was widely acclaimed for its originality in challenging the conventional wisdom on the area.

He traveled widely and became very well known around the world as an activist and scholar. He taught for a time in Tanzania, and later in Jamaica at his alma mater - UWI Mona. Rodney was sharply critical of the middle class for its role in the post-independence Caribbean. He was also a critic of capitalism and argued for a socialist development template.[1] When the Jamaican government, led by prime minister Hugh Shearer, banned him, in October 1968, from ever returning to the country, because of his advocacy for the working poor in that country, riots broke out, eventually claiming the lives of several people and causing millions of dollars in damages. These riots, which started on October 16, 1968, are now known as the Rodney Riots, and they triggered an increase in political awareness across the Caribbean, especially among the Afrocentric Rastafarian sector of Jamaica, documented in his book, The Groundings With My Brothers.

Rodney became a prominent Pan-Africanist, and was important in the Black Power movement in the Caribbean and North America. While living in Dar es Salaam he was influential in developing a new centre of African learning and discussion.

Rodney's most influential book was How Europe Underdeveloped Africa, published in 1972. In it he described an Africa that had been consciously exploited by European imperialists, leading directly to the modern underdevelopment of most of the continent. The book became enormously influential as well as controversial.

Michael Manley

This period of struggle resulted in many people being beaten in the streets by the police, who were forced to maintain the status quo. Jamaica did not escape the wrath of this era and it provided a fertile ground for someone who could galvanize the people to rail against the establishment.

In came Michael Manley, he assumed the leadership of the PNP in a bruising contest for the leadership of the party, which was relinquished by his father Norman Manley, who later became a National Hero. Michael Manley was a populist, a very charismatic and handsome man. He had many Jamaican women drooling over him.

He was educated at Oxford with a degree in Economics. His father, whom he succeeded for the leadership of the PNP, was one of the best known lawyers in the country. They were from the privileged class, but Michael like his father before him, was able to convince the Jamaican people that they represented the black underclass and in some instances they even convinced the people that they too were black. That was achieved, despite the fact that they were as white as snow.

Michael Manley got married to a black Jamaican woman, Beverly Anderson. This was despised by many black Jamaican women and was even more hated by the white upper-class. It was puzzling to many of the more liberated black women as to why that reaction should come from their own, but the Willie Lynch Syndrome was solid after so many years. Beverly was never accepted by Manley's friends and the gazes she received from her peers were even more startling with hatred. Black-toned women thought that she was too dark for Manley and the white upper-class thought that Manley betrayed them by marrying outside his race.

There were many people who thought that Michael married Bev in order to be more politically palatable to the Jamaican people. There were many jobs that dark-skinned people could not get in the civil service and the private sector. To get a job in the bank as a teller was almost impossible. The farther removed from the frontline they were, the better it felt to the people in the status quo. These were the people who were direct descendants of the plantocracy or those who were half-white and who thought that they had a god-given right to rule over blacks; probably marrying Beverly would help to change that perspective, and that was what Manley was about. He was able to convince those disaffected women that his marriage was OK and he cemented in the minds of the populace that he was a 'black' Jamaican.

Prior to becoming the leader of his party, Michael was president of one of the most powerful trade unions in the country, it was also founded by his father. He had a powerful platform on which to launch his political career. He was able to tap into the disenchantment of the majority poor people and despite the impressive growth levels in the economy, Michael was able to use his charisma to galvanize the people and was swept into power as Prime Minister in 1972, just a short three years after assuming the leadership of his party.

The landslide election victory emboldened him to make revolutionary changes in the social structures of the society. Those changes would put him in direct confrontation with the ruling class and would later have devastating consequences for the economy. He introduced sweeping legislations, such as Maternity Leave Pay for women.

He instituted free education for everyone up to university level; but he warmed the hearts of Jamaicans even more by introducing a law to ban the practice of discrimination against people who were born out of wedlock and were called Bastards. This act allowed him to be given god-like status, as most Jamaicans were born out of wedlock and therefore were considered Bastards.

While he was advancing the social agenda, he was alienating the business class. The economy began to deteriorate and the plantocracy were trembling in their boots. They complained about the direction in which the country was heading and Manley responded by inviting them to take one of the three flights out of Jamaica that left to Miami on a daily basis. Many of those persons accepted the offer, and with them a huge amount of foreign currency fled the country. The Net International Reserves that Manley inherited as Prime Minister were completely gone and he set up the Financial Intelligence Unit to seize foreign currency from individuals leaving the country and to place them in jail. This Gestapo-like unit did not stop them and the people used whatever means necessary, to get their monies out of the country. They fled in droves as if a natural disaster had taken place. Many household helpers and gardeners who worked for that upper and middle-class group were suddenly out of work.

Manley sensing that those working class people now being out of jobs could cause widespread hunger and riots, immediately implemented an emergency jobs program. It was known as "crash program" or "bollo wuk" and involved people sweeping the streets and cutting roadside bushes. That kind of work would today be called a stimulus program. There were thousands of people employed under this program and it encouraged many people to sit idly on the streets on a daily basis and then collect their pay at the end of the week. There was hardly any supervision of these people and many stayed home and still got paid. Of course there was no production to back this move, and as broke as the country was, the government was forced to print money to pay the workers. Inflation followed and discontent was creeping into Manley's popularity.

The people who fled on the 'three flights a day', as it became known, left their large mansions behind and political activists associated with the PNP occupied them and claimed ownership. Many others sold their homes at peppercorn rates and took refuge in Miami and New York in the United States.

Cold War

During the turmoil taking place in the country Manley formed a close relationship with the Soviet Union and Cuba and he took a socialist path. At one point during the 'cold war' he became a vice president of Socialist International- an organization aligned with the communist countries around the world. He antagonized our powerful neighbor to the north-the United States with his powerful rhetoric of socialism. He was visited by Secretary Henry Kissinger and told to calm down but Manley was stubborn and he refused to listen to the 'capitalists'.

This was to prove disastrous for Manley and the Jamaican people. The economy went into a precipitous fall aided and abetted by the Central Intelligence Agency (CIA). The entire reserves of the central bank were used up and the Jamaican Dollar that was superior in value to the US Dollar when Manley took power, started losing its value. The oil price shocks of the 1970's did not help, and caused Manley to seek the assistance of the International Monetary Fund (IMF). The conditions imposed upon him by the fund, forced him to cut back significantly on his social agenda and he had to seek more support from his socialist friends. Cuba responded very well with the building of schools, training of workers, and they helped in supplying doctors and nurses to assist in our undermanned hospitals.

The role played by the CIA, the most powerful spy agency in the world, in destabilizing the government should not be underestimated. They aligned with the opposition, JLP, led by a white

American born Jamaican known as Edward Seaga. He received all the funding and support that he needed from the CIA and it was just a matter of time that Manley would wilt under the pressure of a powerful external force and the bold resilience and toughness of Seaga.

Manley's tenure as prime minister from 1972-1980 was the most tumultuous period in the nation since slavery was abolished. Crime raged out of hand, forcing Manley to introduce several emergency measures. He declared a State of Emergency; he introduced the Gun Court Act, which saw trials being held in secret for anyone charged with a gun crime. The Suppression of Crimes Act was also implemented. That gave the police and military sweeping powers to detain people for very long periods without a court appearance. The State of Emergency of 1976 resulted in many persons from the JLP being taken into custody for indefinite periods. Prominent among those were Perneal Charles and Babsy Grange. Manley accused them of being subversive elements and plotting to overthrow the elected government. There was a general election in 1976 and Manley, having some powerful people in the JLP locked away, was able to win another landslide victory at the polls.

The enforcers of the JLP and PNP were brought to the forefront and they engaged in pitch gun battles against each other. Entire communities were held under siege and the security forces in the middle, terrified for their lives and also their jobs. The weapons that were used by the criminal enforcers were much more powerful than those in the hands of the security forces. To come out on the wrong side of the political divide could end up with members of the security forces losing their jobs or transferred to a rural area as punishment.

There was no honeymoon for Manley in his second term and things became even dicier in the ensuing four years. This culminated into a near civil war between the

PNP and JLP, which caused over eight hundred people to be murdered in 1980 because of political violence. Ordinary citizens were now fleeing the country out of fear, to escape the war zone that Jamaica had become.

The turbulence of the Michael Manley era had the entire country wondering what would be next. The country was bewildered and the nation was in a state of shock. Businesses were not able to plan, and decisions were taken by the government overnight that would adversely affect their viability.

The Green Bay Massacre

Any mention of Michael Manley's reign as prime minister of Jamaica of the 1970's will not be truly reflected unless the "Green Bay Massacre" is mentioned. **The Green Bay Massacre** was a covert operation carried out by Special Forces of the Jamaican Government on January 5, 1978, in which five Jamaica Labour Party supporters were shot dead. The operation entailed the luring of the men into an ambush at the Green Bay Firing Range by members of the Military Intelligence Unit which was and still is a covert operational wing of the Jamaica Defense Force.

The victims all hailed from the Higholborn Street and Gold Street areas of the JLP stronghold Southside community in downtown Kingston. They were identified as being too closely linked to the opposition Jamaica Labour Party and were singled out as being prime targets for neutralization by members of the leading **Peoples National Party**. The Military Intelligence Unit (M.I.U) of the Jamaican army which was headed by Lt. Col Desmond Edwards was required by government members to take "all reasonable steps" to ensure removal either overtly or covertly of anyone who was deemed to be a threat to the Islands' security and to the smooth running of the PNP government.

The operation was executed by undercover agents of the Military Intelligence Unit going into the Southside Community and infiltrating the Southside's "POW Posse" which was a local gang operating in the area led by the now deceased Franklyn Allen aka "Chubby Dread". There were fourteen men in this gang who were originally targeted for neutralization. The men were promised guns and jobs in the military if they cooperated with the Government. The

men, needing the arms and funding, agreed; and in the early hours of January 5, 1978 an army ambulance driven by an MIU operative picked them up at the intersection of Higholborn Street and Port Royal Street, then headed west towards Port Henderson, Saint Catherine where the Green Bay artillery range is located. On arrival at the Military Base, the men were led out to a section of the range where they were given strict instructions not to move as they would be picked up by other persons who would take care of their work requirements and supply them with arms. As soon as the MIU operatives drove off, a specially selected team of snipers from the JDF, led by Major Ian Robinson was lying in ambush in the nearby hills. The soldiers were armed with L8 General Purpose Machine Guns (GPMG), L2A2 Self Loading Rifles and Sterling Sub-Machine Guns. On the receipt of a pre-arranged signal from one of the MIU operatives which was the firing of a single shot from his Browning 9mm pistol, the sniper team opened fire on the group of men from their nest in the hills. Five men fell dead under the hail of gunfire and the remainder fled into nearby bushes. At least one entered the Bay and was rescued by a passing fishing boat.

The official report released by the Military stated that the men were shot dead after they were surprised by soldiers doing target practice on the JDF firing range. This report did not stick as the people of Southside demonstrated to protest against the killings. An official inquiry and Coroners' Inquest was later held in the Spanish Town Coroner's Court where a jury found that the sniper team felt threatened by the men when they opened fire, so no one was held criminally responsible for these deaths. The Jamaica Labour Party refused the verdict but did nothing to bring the perpetrators to justice when they were elected on October 30, 1980. The Michael Manley led PNP has always disavowed knowledge of the covert action that took the lives of the men and said it was purely a military operation that was later justified. The incident is considered one of the worst acts of brutality in Jamaican History and is still condemned by members of the Jamaican populace to this day. Several changes have now been made in the operational and administrative functions of the JDF to prevent similar incidents. As a direct result of this act of state brutality, over 1,400 persons were murdered in Jamaica between 1978-1980 when the Michael Manley led PNP was defeated by the opposition JLP led by Edward George Phillip Seaga who ruled until 1989 when he lost the General elections. Southside is still a volatile area with frequent outbreaks of political violence and turf war since the occurrence of this incident and Jamaica is still suffering from tribalism up to this day.

People at the highest level of the society inferred that 'no angels died at Green Bay'. That was a statement similar to what was said by former Prime Minister Hugh Shearer in the 1960's after a demonstration was broken up by the police and citizens were beaten. He said, "What is wrong with a few broken skulls in the birth of a nation?"

The tradition was set, and the people were convinced that violence had to be a way of life for the country. It did not dawn on the leaders that they had to break the back of violence after our independence from Britain in 1962. We have had a history during the days of slavery as one of the most violent set of slaves in the region. It was said that the slave traders would take the more docile slaves to the Eastern Caribbean and the violent ones to Haiti and Jamaica.

If that account was accurate, it could probably explain why a country such as Barbados is so calm but on the other hand there is so much turmoil where the violent slaves were placed. There were several violent uprisings on the sugar plantations in Jamaica during slavery and it is well documented how the Maroons whipped the British forces in Jamaica into submission and forced the Governor to sign a peace treaty and gave the Maroons autonomy over their governance.

The slaves of Haiti also rose up against the French and engaged in a violent revolution, resulting in them being the first Black Country in this hemisphere to gain their independence from the Europeans. The struggles of these violent slaves in the Western Caribbean resulted in the abolition of the slave trade in the Caribbean and later in the United States.

The "few broken skulls in the birth of a nation" statement legalized state terrorism and saw police and soldiers beat and kill innocent citizens on a regular basis. There is no respect for the sanctity of life, unless you are a convicted murderer, where the government has refused to put in the necessary mechanisms to carry out the course of the law, which is death by hanging.

Edward Seaga

We now come to the much maligned and most hated person to have led the country. Edward Phillip George Seaga, who was born in the United States but renounced his citizenship from the United States in order to play an active role in affairs of his, adopted country, Jamaica. He went on to play a very active part in the governance of the country. He served in the legislature as one of the founding members of the country's road to independence. He served in many ministerial capacities and was considered to be a very good manager. He was however viewed with suspicion by many persons. They thought that he was too ambitious and wanted to be prime minister and they did not like it that he was white. He too married a black Jamaican woman-Mitzie. He was feared by the establishment because he was no pushover and that was not to their liking.

Seaga was a determined politician and he would get his way by any means necessary. He realized that to achieve his ambition he would have to carve out a permanent seat under our Westminster system of government, which was enshrined in our constitution by the British.

He used the excuse that the PNP had established secured communities that the JLP could not penetrate and that in order for the JLP to survive, it had to establish its own. This kind of secured environment was later described by the late Professor Carl Stone as Garrison Constituency and later extended to Garrison communities. Seaga set about bulldozing a section of West Kingston, then known as Back-A-Wall. He displaced many people in the process. Those that were aligned to the PNP had to stay out permanently and they moved over into the neighboring parish of St. Catherine to a place that was later known as Sufferers Heights. Those who were his supporters were housed

into brand new homes in what became known as Tivoli Gardens and which was named off the famed garden in Copenhagen, Denmark. He added all the amenities that a community needed and the people who moved there had never had such glorious lifestyle. They became fiercely loyal to him and he had over forty years of unbroken representation of that garrison constituency.

In later years Tivoli Gardens was described by the head of the military, Rear Admiral Hardley Lewin as the 'mother of all garrisons'. The community frequently engages the police and military in high-pitch gun battles, sometimes lasting several days. It is off-limits to the security forces and appears to be self-governed. A walk through the community will reveal an eerie sense of peace and quietness. An unaccompanied outsider enters at his own peril and the very mention of the name Tivoli Gardens, drives fear in the hearts of many people throughout the country. It is well kept and clean compared to the rest of Kingston and the other garrison communities.

Seaga like other holders of garrison seats have managed to miraculously garner over one hundred percent of the registered voters in those constituencies on Election Day. If you were not able to vote within an hour of the opening of polls, then, 'no problem', someone else would cast your vote for you in very open voting. They would sometimes drop in a little dribbles for the opposing party as a consolation.

There have been several dons throughout the JLP dominated garrison communities, but all those dons would be answerable to the ultimate don who is always from Tivoli Gardens.

It operates like a headquarters of the JLP, it has the most delegates of all constituencies and those members who wish to move up into the hierarchy of the party must have a relationship with Tivoli and pay homage to the Don of the area, who acts as an overlord. By and large the same kind of incestuous practices exist in the PNP.

There is something different with how Seaga controlled his garrison. It is very glaring that he was the ultimate ruler and was so depicted in the newspaper cartoons as a don wearing a big gold chain around his neck and issuing orders. He had had an iron-clad control over his party. If anyone in his party stepped out of line or tried to challenge him for leadership, it would result in the end of that person's political career. The likes of very bright men such as Frank Phipps and Ian Ramsay are stark reminders. As party leader he was feared, despised, and also loved by many. He was also not afraid to take on the establishment but was a capitalist at heart.

Seaga is mainly characterized as a builder of institutions such as the Urban Development Corporation (UDC), but most Jamaicans see him as a warrior and a defender of 'badmanism'. This view was promoted by his political opponents, the PNP and to a great extent the media. He did not help his image when on several occasions he confronted the security forces when they carried out raids in Tivoli Gardens, or when he perceived that the police perpetrated any illegal action against his constituents. He has a complex personality and the lead up to the general election of 1980 will dissect some of his complexities. After the 1976 General Election, in which many of his frontline leaders and alleged enforcers were jailed, and which he lost to Manley under a State of Emergency, he was determined to fight to the end to save Jamaica's democracy. He was of the firm view, and with his lust for power, held the belief that Manley was taking the country down a communist

path. He would have played out to be the rockiest period in Jamaica's history and entrenched the division of the people along party lines.

Being in the forefront of the fight of his life and that of the country, he resolutely mobilized the Jamaican people against Manley's socialist ideas. Backed up with fierce firepower from his enforcers, he was able to take the gunfight and the ideological warfare into the hearts of his political opponents. The JLP enforcers seemed to have possessed the more powerful weapons and though Manley had men trained in Cuba in military tactics and were known as brigadistas; they were outgunned and outmaneuvered by the heavily armed Labourites.

During the campaign leading up to the 1980 election, Manley's party used the state-owned buses to transport its supporters to meetings around the country and they became prime targets of the Labourite gunmen. The buses were frequently fired upon and PNP supporters were often killed or injured. People were killed at will when they went to political meetings and wore their party colors. To wear green, which was the color of the JLP or orange colored clothes, which was the color of the PNP, even if you did not belong to a political party was tantamount to committing suicide. You would likely be killed if you ventured outside of a garrison which did not support the color clothes you were wearing.

The country was extremely tense, the people were terrified and the pressure from Seaga was relentless. There were work stoppages and schools were disrupted in many areas due to shootouts between rival gunmen. There were food shortages; many thought they were artificially imposed, as Seaga's allies in the business sector helped him to tighten the screws on the Manley regime. Basic food items were sold as a pair and populace termed it as 'married'. For example, if you wanted rice you also had to buy some salt fish, which increased the sales of the businesses but placed severe burdens on the consumers. The wealthy that remained in Jamaica were able to go to Miami on the weekends to do their shopping, and hence did not suffer any shopping indignities.

The shortages forced Jamaicans to be innovative, and Manley forced into a corner of diminished foreign exchange, exalted the people to adopt what he called 'self-reliance'. He encouraged them to grow what they ate and to eat what they grew. Many backyard gardens were commissioned, especially by PNP supporters, also known as Comrades, but not many lasted, as people got used to the idea of getting paid while sitting on the streets. Many of the Comrades felt that self-reliance was a part of the prophecy that was preached by their own 'Joshua', a biblical prophet and was a name given to Michael Manley on the campaign trail.

People were able to survive, but their ability to withstand the pressure was waning and the 1979 gas riots led by the JLP's Michael Williams, after Manley announced a tax on gasoline sales, shut down the entire country for a few days. There were fires burning on the streets, factories were locked down, no transportation was available and Jamaica became a ghost town, except for the JLP enforcers who controlled the streets. This forced Manley to announce the election for October of 1980, an eight month period, a very long period between the announcement and the actual election date. Under the Jamaican constitution, only the prime minister can call an election within the stipulated five years period in which a government was elected. The period was bloody and though Manley still had the love of the people; Seaga's tenacity was respected and the people

had high hopes of enjoying a better life under Seaga and hoped that money would jingle in their pockets as he promised.

Thepeoplewiltedunderthepressure and Manley was swept out of power in a massive landslide defeat in which Seaga billed as 'Deliverance', a biblical reference to Moses delivering the Israelites. Bells rang out in the streets and echoed into every crevice and corner of Jamaica. The bell, the symbol of the JLP was music to ears of the people and was a welcome relief to the powers in Washington who bankrolled the JLP's victory. Those who were still in the corner of Manley also had to ring bells out of fear that they would be attacked if they did not do so. JLP enforcers quickly rushed into housing developments built by the PNP and chased out the home owners and captured their properties. One such development was Tawes Pen in Spanish Town, which today is still a stronghold of the Jamaica Labour Party.

Seaga ascended to the 'throne' of Prime Minister, which he knew he was destined for and was possibly ordained to achieve. Though he had the burning desire to change the lives of the people for the better; he seemed like someone who would do so by any means necessary. After the election he tried to get the country settled down and to try and revive the economy. He was still in the throes of the IMF and had to impose some of the stiffest austerity measures imposed by the Fund and which Manley strenuously resisted. Seaga soon found out that the IMF was not as he characterized it during the campaign, "Is Manley's Fault", but was now an albatross hanging around his neck. He had to quickly cut back on social services that Manley had instituted and his seventy-four percent popularity that brought him to power was torpedoing off the hills of the Blue Mountains and into the depths of the pit latrines used by many Jamaicans.

He was soon to become the most despised person in Jamaica and the people quickly resumed their love-affair with their prophet 'Joshua'. With his 'rod of correction' wanted him to return to 'fix' things. Within eighteen months the people were ready to see the back of Seaga. Ronald Reagan saved the day for him, when in 1983 he invaded the tiny Caribbean island of Grenada, to 'restore' democracy after the government was deposed in a coup by Marxist elements. Seaga backed him solidly by sending soldiers from the Jamaica Defense Force to join the United States military.

This was a big boost for Seaga, because the Jamaican people were vehemently against communism and they felt that Reagan was correct to invade the island and that Seaga did the noble thing to support the efforts. Seaga's popularity went back up the Blue Mountain hills and he used the opportunity to call a snap general election. Manley and his party was caught completely off-guard and refused to contest the election on the grounds that Seaga had promised that he would not call an election on the voter's list used for the 1980 election, lest it would disenfranchise one hundred thousand Jamaicans. Despite the PNP's 'trumpeting' from Manley, Seaga went ahead with the election and Manley realizing that he had absolutely no chance of winning; indeed, carried out his threat of not contesting. Seaga ended up controlling the entire parliament. He was able to kick aside Members of Parliament from his party with whom he did not find favor and replaced them with loyalists. He however, and much to his credit, used the Senate (the upper chamber) of parliament to appoint some independent-minded people. He could have used the control he had to bring about the most fundamental changes possible to the constitution, which I think the country desperately needed, but constrained himself in doing so. He was not able to win the hearts and minds of the Jamaican people, but he was respected as prime minister, for managing the affairs of the country in a capable and pragmatic manner.

Jamaicans were not in favor of his austerities and they also did not like his association with Jim Brown, the Tivoli Gardens don. It was claimed that Jim Brown, went into Rema in 1984 and allegedly killed seven people. It was reported that the men had betrayed the JLP and defected to the PNP. Jim Brown was charged for the murder of the men but was acquitted by the jury at a Supreme Court trial. Seaga and other Cabinet ministers went to Tivoli Gardens to drink a celebratory beer with Brown after his acquittal.

That scene and the spirit of his leadership of the JLP as well as his anemic PR team had him cast in a bad light up to the time of his retirement from active politics. Many people prefer to remember his sidelining of Ian Ramsay, Frank Phipps, Perneal Charles and Douglas Vaz, very notable figures and potential threats to his leadership than to remember his remarkable leadership in building of the UDC, Human Employment and Resource Training (HEART) and his beautifying of the parks and cleansing of the markets. He was able to stabilize and grow the Jamaican economy and maintained a stable exchange rate. One of his most remarkable shows of leadership was his restoration of the country in record time after the passage of Hurricane Gilbert in September 1988. He was voted out of power ina general election five months after the hurricane; with his erstwhile opponent again Michael Manley.

PJ Patterson

Michael 'Joshua' Manley returned to power, transformed from his bush jackets, and now sporting business suits and a different ideology of capitalism; re-engaged the capitalists and provided them with everything that they asked. He had as his deputy PJ Patterson, his longtime friend and party organizer and Manley's absolute heir apparent. PJ was given the ministry of Development and Planning and his colleague Seymour 'Foggy' Mullings was given the Ministry of Finance. Mullings quickly proved to be a 'foggy' figure at the Finance Ministry and with the exchange rate slipping he was replaced by Patterson. PJ in his new role as finance minister, increased money supply and had interest rates running at somewhere between sixty to one hundred percent. Businesses were in a tizzy and did not know where to turn. Banks started investing in everything that they could get their hands on. They were investing in farming and hotels, and non-banking activities, but there were no laws against them doing it so and they had more money than they could use. PJ created the illusion that we were creating wealth but he was not to last very long into that ministry either. In came what became known as the 'Shell Waiver Scandal'.

In a classic case of cronyism, PJ and his close friend Howard Hamilton, the general manager of Shell gas in Jamaica, made an arrangement for Hamilton's company to benefit from a tax waiver on the importation of a new unleaded octane gas into the country. The gas would have attracted about thirty seven million dollars in customs duty but PJ as Finance Minister waived the duty without taking the matter before the Cabinet. Someone leaked the matter to the press and it became a major distraction. Manley, as Prime Minister, was livid and called a series of emergency

Cabinet meetings, and backed solidly by Hugh Small, Manley's blue-eyed boy, he fired PJ from the Cabinet. Patterson sounded the famous warning that General McArthur made, "I Shall Return". Many thought those were hollow words, but keen political observers were on the lookout for the quiet unassuming PJ. Manley appointed Hugh Small to be Finance Minister and he set about to repair the ills of Patterson in that ministry. There was the issue of the excess liquidity in the financial system and that was a priority for Small. He had a very difficult time as Finance Minister because PJ's friends in the Cabinet were still mad with him for his role in having Patterson fired and he was constantly given the cold-shoulder.

PJ's Return

Within a few months of his firing PJ honored the McArthur doctrine and returned in fine style. Manley became ill and resigned as party leader and prime minister, and PJ whipped his former cabinet colleague, the populist Portia Simpson for the contest of party leader and PJ ultimately became Prime Minister. PJ quickly brushed off the scars of the scandal that had earlier bedeviled him and set about portraying a public image as being a consensus builder. As the new Prime Minister he brought back his challenger in the leadership contest to a prominent post in the Cabinet and also retained Hugh Small as Finance Minister. It was suspected that he was quietly undermining Small, who had supported Portia in the leadership contest. Small felt the heat and quickly got out of the kitchen. He resigned from the ministry and became a backbencher.

The Cabinet was thrown in a quandary as there was no one considered suitable in its rank to replace Small. Under the Westminster system of government the Chancellor of the Exchequer or in our case the Finance Minister, must be a member of the House of Representatives. PJ's choice was a party operative and university lecturer, Dr Omar Davies, who was later given the nick-name, Dr Clueless. PJ asked Bobby Jones the Member of Parliament for South West St Andrew also known as 'Jungle', a PNP garrison community to resign from the seat and trigger a by-election. The election was held and as is customary in a garrison community, the party that controls the area wins handsomely. Omar was elected or selected, if you wish, and took his place in the parliament as Finance Minister.

PJ as prime minister was a pragmatist and would do whatever it took to remain in power.

He was the first prime minister to win three consecutive terms in government. He seemed to be able to outsmart his opponents at will, and it was much easier because of the fact that his opposition was Edward Seaga, who had become unelectable. PJ surrounded himself with loyalists and his leadership was never challenged. After the leadership contest with Portia Simpson ended, PJ set about rebuilding the party in his own image and everybody fell in line.

Omar Davies and PJ were inseparable during PJ's reign. For the fourteen years that Omar presided over the Finance Ministry, he borrowed, plundered and imposed on Jamaica, the highest level of voodoo economics in this part of the hemisphere. They together ran up a debt of over one trillion dollars. The dollar declined in value from $7.50 to $68.00 vis-a-vis the United States dollar. There was less than one percent average increase in overall GDP. The borrowing of money on the overseas capital market was hailed as great successes for the government's macroeconomic policies, but they constantly forgot the deleterious effect it had on the micro sector and made the poor that they loved, so much poorer.

Industries moved their businesses overseas, especially to Trinidad and the Trinidadians came roaring in with their dollars to buy up what was left of us.

PJ was able to keep the people quiet by boxing Seaga's opposition party in a corner and also offering some niceties to the people. The advent of cellular phones became widespread in the world, and Jamaicans with their fascination for talking and gossip were right in the mix. Cellular licenses were auctioned off after PJ Patterson's telecommunications minister Phillip Paulwell had the existing monopoly of Cable & Wireless broken up. The national pastime of talking now became a culture.

Jamaicans riding donkeys were chatting on the cell phone, men pushing handcarts for their livelihood had up to two cell phones and one government minister boasted that men were now able to call themselves from one phone to the next. PJ himself was bold enough to boast that men had many cell phones and cars and also 'nuff gals'. He had the taxes on the importation of motor vehicles lowered, allowing many more persons at the lower strata of society to be able to purchase a car for the first time. Many young people were able to feel hopeful and with the increased building of more houses for young people, PJ held unto office without any serious threats.

There were many scandals which rocked his administration, but with a weak opposition and his ability to deflect scrutiny from important issues, he was able to maintain a steady hold on government. As a longtime stalwart of the party's propaganda machinery, he was able to dictate the message. His ability to maintain the loyalty of his party rested with him being their staunchest backers. If there were any suggestions of impropriety on their part, they could rely on PJ Patterson to be rock-solid behind them.

One of the most glaring failures of the PJ Patterson Administration was his failure in controlling crime in the country. He and his National Security Minister K.D. Knight presided over a massive increase in the country's murder rate. Knight was later shifted to the Ministry of Foreign Affairs and Peter Phillips had to pick up the slack. He was a capable minister but the rot had set in so badly, it was extremely difficult for him to tame the rampant murder rate

and was not as successful as he was used to being in other ministries.

Under PJ's leadership there was a feeling of free for all that permeated the society. The gunmen were allowed to run rampant, taxis and mini-buses were allowed to take control of the streets and the general lack of discipline cast a sense of hopelessness in the country. Law-abiding citizens felt threatened and gave way to those who intimidated others. Peter Phillips himself intimated that, the people who played by the rules, were the ones who got shafted.

Values & Attitudes

PJ to his credit introduced a values and attitudes program, with the objective of bringing back some civility to the society. It was a bold initiative but pundits have indicated that it was undermined by PJ himself, who ignored the web of corruption that engulfed his stewardship. He was let down by his Finance Minister, he had genuine intentions of lifting up the poor, but with the lack of resources due to the lack of growth, he was unable to satisfy his election promises. He however, was able to bring about land reform policies and Operation Pride was well received in helping to provide housing solutions to very many people. Operation Pride was a land reform housing program intended to benefit mainly the poor and middle class. It was quickly hijacked by PNP party operatives such as Danhai Williams and Skeng Don. They were the main persons involved in clearing the lands, putting in infrastructure and in some instances, selecting people who received benefits.

The government advanced money to the projects and individuals went about setting up provident societies and making down-payments to assist with the infrastructural phase of the housing projects. Contracts were awarded to Danhai and Skeng Don who were well connected to the ruling party and in many instances they delivered projects on time. Unlike other government projects that were mired in delays, their connections with the underworld prevented any kinds of extortion and the usual flare-ups on construction projects on the island.

There were instances of money being awarded to contractors to complete projects in the scheme but they failed to deliver. Civil servants whose jobs it were to check on projects and make verification for payments were in on corrupt deals with the contractors to sign off on work done.

Payments were made where no work was done and was brought to public attention by the Auditor General, whose job is to ferret out cases of misappropriation of government funds. Police investigations followed and some persons were arrested, including Danhai Williams and charged with fraud. The government minister who had portfolio responsibility for the project, Dr Karl Blythe was fired from his job, in what became known as the Operation Pride Scandal.

In spite of the action taken by PJ in this episode of corruption, the people had already branded his administration as corrupt. Phillip Paulwell, who was his Technology Minister, was fingered in another scandal where investors from abroad were given millions of dollars of taxpayer's money from the Intech Fund, to set up technology projects in St Thomas and Portmore in St Catherine. These advances were supposed to have provided thousands of new jobs. No jobs materialized, as the 'investors' left with the money without any form of accountability. Again, this was brought to the Prime Minister PJ Patterson's attention and he dismissed criticisms of the minister as youthful exuberance. No one was fired and that situation among many others defined the PJ Patterson Administration.

Omar Davies

Omar's lack of economic growth dwarfed the resources available for PJ to realize his mandate; there were several young people leaving school without the requisite educational level to compete in society; many of these young people turned to crime and when confronted with the issue in his own constituency, Omar Davies sounded the warning that the young men were irredeemable.

With no growth in the economy, Omar was still able to amass a sizeable reserve in the Bank of Jamaica, which he often boasted about. Not one red cent of that was money earned from production, it was all borrowed money, on which the country had to pay the highest interest rate of any country on the entire planet. He was characterized by many commentators as a father who had money stashed away but had his children go to bed hungry. Businesses became fat on the high interest rate regime, operated by Omar. Companies that were in production stopped producing. They instead moved their money into government paper. The government continued to tax the people more and more in order to satisfy our debt repayment obligations. Who could fault those companies for making that shift, when they could earn fifty percent profit in securities without any risk?

1999 Gas Riots

The 'Gas Riots' of April 16-21, 1999, which I personally orchestrated along with my friend Wayne Leahong and Lorane Ferguson, placed some brakes on the parasitic taxation tendencies of Omar. We went into Half-Way-Tree and blocked the intersection of South Odeon Avenue and Constant Spring Road, causing traffic to be blocked for miles and had thousands of people join us. We controlled the streets that Friday and kept the momentum on the airwaves over the weekend. All broke loose the following Monday when the JLP was able to mobilize their garrisons to overwhelm the streets and caused a complete lockdown of the country.

It all started when I was in Portmore that Thursday evening April 15, and was listening to Omar's Budget Presentation. I was stunned at what I was hearing and I called Leahong who was at a Kiwanis meeting at the Spanish Town Health Centre. I went there to meet him and we had a discussion about what the implications of the taxation on gas would be. I told him that I was not going to take it lying down and I wanted him to join me. He had indicated to me a few months before that he wanted to join me in a demonstration because he had learned of a 'one man' demonstration that I'd done a few months before. He was however, reluctant to join me out of a tinge of fear, because he had not done anything of the sort before. He had thoughts of Bustamante bearing his chest and dared the police to shoot him and he felt that this could be a moment to replicate that. He had shared those sentiments with me months prior and I felt that this was his moment to be a hero. He did not readily commit to be a part of any demonstration.

I then solicited the assistance of my sisters and my eldest sister Marcia readily decided to join me and my younger sister's employee, Narda Brown also decided to take part. We spent the night writing up some placards and decided that Half-Way-Tree was the place to go in order to have the biggest impact. I again contacted Leahong and he said to me, "Shawn you are pushing my button." I acknowledged that I was doing so, and reminded him that this was his desire, and that the moment was now. He told me that he would sleep on it and that I should call him very early in the morning. I called him at 4:30 that Friday morning and asked him if he was ready. He was still reluctant and I told him that I would go without him if he was scared. He took the bait and decided then that he was ready. He hated the idea that I would consider him a coward.

We agreed to meet at the Shell Gas Station at the intersection of Dunrobin Road and Constant Spring Road. I picked up my two female revolutionaries and met Leahong at the agreed spot. He took over the planning from that point and I had no objection. It was obvious to me that he had read some kind of revolutionary propaganda book and he was about to execute what he had read. He told me how I would go across the traffic light from South Odeon Avenue, when the light changed to green, and I would stop in the middle of the road with my pickup and he would stop right behind me with his pickup.

He had earlier called TVJ, which was located at South Odeon Avenue, and told them that something was about to happen outside their gate shortly, and that they should come out. We executed the plan with military precision and within a few minutes the peak hour traffic had backed up for miles. The bravery that Leahong displayed was reminiscent of Bustamante. He tore his shirt open and bore his chest for

the television camera and repeated some words of his idol. The camera caught this half-Chinese guy, heroically standing up for the people and they zeroed in on him. We were quickly joined by hundreds of people who were also enraged with the increases and within minutes, Half-Way-Tree was blocked solidly with people.

Another ally, Lorane Ferguson came on the scene later. We had alerted him earlier that morning about our plan. His arrival sparked frenzy. He came in an executive-looking BMW and with his protruding stomach. The crowd saw a 'big-man' and they were ready to follow him. He shouted "Let's go to Jamaica House" and he headed in the direction of the Prime Minister's office and a significant portion of the crowd moved with him. He was however blocked by the police and never got to Jamaica House.

Wayne Leahong, Lorane Ferguson and I were members of Jamaica's fledgling third party, the National Democratic Movement (NDM). We got on the phone and alerted as many officials of the party as possible. We were joined shortly by Barbara Clarke, a vice president of the NDM; I also remember seeing Peter Townsend among others. Barbara quickly got into activist mode and encouraged us to constantly walk to and fro across the pedestrian crossing, not allowing any vehicles to get by. We had no intention of placing any debris in the road or to burn any tires. Her suggestion was very successful, as there was a complete standstill without any harm to public property. We were later joined by elements of the JLP lead by Prudence Kidd-Deans, who politely asked us to allow her and her supporters, who I suspected she brought with her to join us in our peaceful march across the pedestrian crossing. That pedestrian crossing is the busiest crossing anywhere in Jamaica.

The NDM controlled the streets and we tried desperately to get our leader Bruce Golding to join us. He never appeared. Meanwhile, Omar Davies was having his post-budget press conference and was told by the news media that there were demonstrations on the streets against his increases. He dismissed the protestors and promised that there would not be any roll-back. The Mobile Reserve police led by Senior Superintendent Pusey arrived on the scene in a truck and without warning fired off tear-gas in the crowd and had his men swinging their batons like crazy. I just missed being hit by a policeman. They arrested a few people on the scene and the very brave Lorane Ferguson volunteered to go jail and he too was arrested. The weekend came and the people were simmering.

The JLP had by then mobilized and was ready for a fight. The NDM members were also ready to see the back of PJ, but we had a reluctant leader in Bruce Golding. Seaga's party took over the streets on Monday, April 19, and the tone of everything changed. The roads right across the country was blocked with debris and anything solid that people could lay their hands on. No traffic could travel anywhere and the government was scared.

Not having any seat in the parliament, the NDM was scheduled to have its response to Omar's Budget presentation at the Hilton Hotel in New Kingston and we were worried that our members would not be able to make it to the venue. Wayne Chen, our spokesman on finance was scheduled to speak and he was travelling in from Manchester. Nonetheless, he made it into Kingston and Bruce Golding spoke after him.

We had planned that after the presentation we would

march to Half-Way-Tree. A full ballroom had turned up and the people were in a militant mood. They were ready to take it to PJ. Bruce and Wayne Chen eloquently showcased the NDM's plan as to how to move the country forward and we were ready to engage the government and the official opposition in some kind of power-sharing agreement. After the presentation we thought that we were now going to press our case by having the party leader march to Half-Way-Tree and engage the people. Up to that time the people had associated the NDM with the leadership of the demonstrations. We left out of the Hilton and headed up Knutsford Boulevard with a throng of NDM supporters following Bruce Golding. When we got to the intersection with Trafalgar Road, Bruce turned right onto Trafalgar Road, opposite our planned destination and headed to his office on Braemar Avenue, a short distance away. The NDM leader was scared and we lost the initiative.

Seaga now had the upper hand and a demonstration that was started by the NDM, was now owned by the JLP. PJ Patterson was scared and he called a meeting at Jamaica House with students from the University of the West Indies and you could see him visibly shaking, while addressing them. The wily PJ also got the powerful PSOJ, lead by the respected Peter Moses to come up with a set of alternatives to the taxes that were imposed.

By the end of the third day, the riot was fizzling and PJ had regained the initiative. Seaga was not very well liked and the people were willing to give PJ another chance. He had promised that there were a different set of people in the country who would not take things lying down and that he would listen a lot more to us. The people believed him and the pressure was off. Omar Davies had to eat his words and roll back the taxes on gasoline.

Heather Robinson

My defining insight into the mind of PJ Patterson and how politically raw he would hold onto and handle power, came when the issue of garrison politics reared its head in a constituency controlled by Heather Robinson, a woman who had worked tirelessly, using a lot of her own money to promote PJ Patterson's return to power after he was fired by Manley in the Shell Waiver issue. In the early days of his departure from the Cabinet she managed his campaign and was all over the country handing out PJ t-shirts and PJ memorabilia and drumming up his support. They seemed to know Manley's departure before he announced his retirement.

After PJ became prime minister he rewarded Heather by giving her his support over D.K. Duncan for the newly created constituency of South St. Catherine. She became the Member of Parliament in a by-election, in a strong PNP seat. Heather was very familiar with the area, because it was a part of the constituency a few years earlier controlled by Hugh Small, of which she was the campaign manager. She hit the ground running and had high hopes of changing the lives of her constituents.

She quickly came into conflict with criminal elements in her constituency including the notorious Bulbie and refused to work with them in the fashion that we have come to know as the relationship with Members of Parliament and dons or enforcers. Heather's main goal was to educate the young people in her constituency and to assist the police in ridding her area of 'badmanism'. She refused to give the criminals government contracts and they threatened to remove her from the seat. She sought the assistance of her party leader and prime minister, PJ Patterson, in helping her to rid the area of criminals and dons. There were meetings held with PJ, Heather Robinson, and other leaders of the party. Heather ended up resigning and proclaimed that, "she would not hug up any gunmen."

PJ was consumed with power, more than principle and he threw Heather under the bus. He refused to support a principled woman who wanted to see the breakup of garrison communities and to sideline criminals from their links to political parties. Crime continues unabated and that may have been a defining moment in changing the course of history from the rampant criminality that the country has been experiencing for many years.

HELL IN PARADISE

Crime & Violence

Crime and violence has become a way of life for the Jamaican people. It took on new wheels during the election campaign of 1980. That was the closest we got to a civil war. Each word uttered by Manley was greeted by an opposing and harsher word from Seaga or vice versa. These two foes were bitterly against each other and their large numbers of supporters took on the tone of their leaders. They brought their animosities into their communities, which turned first into stone throwing fights, then it turned into machete fights, then handguns graduated to machine guns and that is where we have been since. The division among the people has percolated inside the homes and many families have broken up as a result. There were sibling rivalries over politics. There were also wives and husbands getting into heated arguments over Manley and Seaga, causing break-ups.

It tore into our communities in the most vicious and savage ways. People could no longer express themselves openly, as they should in a democracy. The enforcers from the city were given homestead in some rural communities and they were the ones who decided which party the community voted for. The people were cowered into fear. They had to whisper to their closest neighbors who their preferred political party or candidate was. This was even more precarious if it was an evenly divided community. People's homes were burned to the ground by the enforcers if they did not submit to their dictates. On the other hand, if you lived in a garrison, you could only support the party of choice and you had to do so openly.

With the dons being in full control, they had to keep a constant flow of new recruits. Many were killed by the police and others by rival party supporters. This forced the dons to go for boys as young as twelve years old. Their indoctrination included shooting and killing stray dogs on the streets and cleaning the don's guns. Their ultimate test was to prove that they could go out of their community and rob and kill someone. It would not matter if the person did not put up any resistance. The goal was to put a notch on that gun loaned to him by the don. Upon successful completion of that mission he would be elevated up the ranks and given bolder missions to tackle. If one of these youngsters were able to rob a policeman or licensed firearm holder and take their guns, he would be propelled into the top echelons of the gang. These youngsters no longer found school to be attractive and many dropped out. Those who remained in school did so only to go to school with his gun to boast to his friends about his new power. Others who attended co-ed schools and displayed rogue behavior got the attention of girls who were either afraid of them or were fascinated by their power and the respect he got from his friends.

The new found 'respect' meant a lot to these guys. They were used to having their mothers and very often their step-fathers bashing them around. In America that would be considered child-abuse, but it is considered normal in Jamaica. They were often beaten savagely by the step-father for youthful transgressions and now found out that with their new 'power', they could no longer be subjected to such beatings. These 12-16 years old kids, increasingly became the breadwinners of the family. Their mothers, who in most instances played the dual role of both parents, were very often unemployed or earned very little. These new 'men' now assumed the role of provider, by going out to rob and kill, to provide food and other essential items for the home, such as clothing and furniture. The mothers in most instances would not be in total agreement with their sons going about life in that way; they would fear for their sons lives, but nevertheless, they would be happy for their new found 'riches' and would eventually become somewhat content with their sons way of life.

The boy's most important role however, was being the protector of the home for his mom and sisters. The don is able to send for any woman in the community that he wishes to sleep with, and they cannot refuse. Many are very young mothers who started having kids from as young as 10-12 years old. If she has a young daughter who was reaching puberty, the don would summon the young girl to be taken to him for his use and her age would not be a factor in his consideration. The mere sight of seeing her young tits protruding from her chest was the only thing considered. The young female girls would sometimes be spared if their brothers were followers of the don and in most instances they had to be in the upper echelons. That would enable him to talk to the don directly, to spare his sister or mother. The young boys in these garrisons who refuse to take part in gang activities are seen as a sissy and they are pushed around in their communities. They are the boys sent to shops to do errands for the dons and their followers.

The young 'gunmen' are also burdened with the responsibility of supporting their girlfriends. These girls are dancehall enthusiasts and they boast among themselves as to who is the 'hottest' and the sexiest and who can dress the skimpiest to visit the dance.

Their attire has to be changed daily and the more costly the clothes, the more respect the young boys earn for being 'good providers'. Rivalry is a common phenomenon of women in the dancehall. It would usually come about when a girlfriend from the crew envies another girlfriend's spectacular outfit from the dance the night prior. Her aim the following day would be to get involved with that girl's boyfriend, so that he could now support her. She would also aim to have him abandon his girlfriend to be with her. The abandoned girlfriend is usually her friend and sometimes considered best friends. She would not want to be outshone and would go to any means to get that guy's support. That would cause many fights and would result in knives being used to slash one or the other across the face from earlobe to the center of the lip and is known as a 'telephone' cut. Acid is another brutal weapon used by many women to disfigure their rivals and would also place fear in the men that they desired and these men would ultimately submit to their wishes. Many young girls usually bore children for the same men and they are called 'mateys'. The young girls are expected to become pregnant by age sixteen or they could be considered to be 'mules'; which refers to the animal that is among the horse family that cannot have offspring.

Irredeemable

Many of the youngsters that Omar Davies considered to be irredeemable were in fact, well described. They had no formal education and if they gave an address from the ghetto to a potential employer, they would not get the job. Many thought that their only alternative was to continue plying their trade of robbing and killing. When not eking out a living for themselves and their families, they would be preparing for battle with the opposing party supporters. Frequent raids into the other's territory would result in some guns being stolen and a few of their opponents killed. That would bring joy and celebration to their community as well as preparation for when the enemy would strike back.

The police reports that seventy two percent of all crimes in the country emanate from the garrison communities controlled by the two parties. Though these parties can solidly depend on their garrisons to back them when they need people mobilized, they have largely ignored the people. Many of the people living there exist in filth and squalor. Their roads are dirty and they lack jobs. Some of the schools in these areas are some of the worst in the country. The people are flatly taken for granted. The buildings are unkempt and their toilets are black plastic bags, better known as 'scandal bags', which are used for depositing feces and then thrown out of the high rise buildings and end up into the common areas of the yard for the dogs to drag them all around. There are instances when there is no running water and their only possible source of water is to break open a fire hydrant.

The people are kept into this situation in order for the politicians to keep their lofty seats in parliament, for the big businesses who depend on government help to retain their positions, all at the expense of the poor and middle class. The people then look to migration as a possible way out of their predicament. They see friends and family who take the trek abroad suddenly sending them pictures of their houses and cars and most of them wait for that day when they too will get to 'farring' for that new lifestyle. They are happy being the beneficiaries of barrels packed with food and clothes and most importantly a few guns are hidden among the goods. The gun exporters are given respect when they return home to Jamaica because they allowed the dons and semi dons to 'hold off' the corners.

Although crime and violence has been a way of life in Jamaica since the Europeans captured the country from the Indians and continued throughout slavery; the modern day violence has done untold harm to the citizens and has left blistering scars on the minds of many young persons. The country accepts as many as three million tourists each year but there are many more that stay away because of the sordid reputation of our crime problems and gun running's. The country is robbed of those valuable foreign currency and money that could certainly redeem many of the young men who have very limited alternatives. Violence is pervasive in many of our high schools. The government seems incapable of dealing with the situation. There are feuds over girls, feuds over dancehall artistes, gang rivalries, political conflicts and a general sense that the society is drifting towards anarchy. The politicians have given up hope and so have many of the people. When walking on the streets the citizens can become very scared. There are men perched on walls and on sidewalks all over, who stare straight into your eyes with the intention to detect fear. Once that fear is detected, then it's time for them to move in, to beg you something or attack you mainly with knives and guns. If you are a woman you may be raped and if you offer any resistance you may be killed.

Our town centers are controlled by hoodlums who work on behalf of the dons. They extort money from businesses and they control the transportation centers where drivers and conductors have to pay dues in order to operate. Two of the most well known gangs at the moment are the One Order Gang, which is aligned to the Jamaica Labour Party and the Klansman Gang, aligned to the People's National Party. They are both based in St. Catherine, but have been extending themselves into other parishes. These gangs are run like multinational corporations. They supply guns to surrogates in different communities, who employ youths to go out to rob and kill and the money handed over to the dons who then pay the henchmen. If there is any word of deception in the amount handed over, it could result in death for the underling. The gangs supplement their incomes by being 'sub-contractors' for firms who win major government contracts or they get smaller contracts from the party that they are affiliated with. As a matter of course, the reputable contract winners must dole out parts of the contract to the underground sub-contractor in order for the work to go ahead. Most jobs on private or government projects will not be allowed to take place, unless a don is involved. He must be paid for himself as well as each worker he supplies to the project. He pays occasional visits to the project site and meets with the builder, owner or the point man. He is able to ensure that there is no disruption to the work schedule, and for that he takes in a hefty payment for security. The don holds the sway between the politician and the community because he is with the people on a day to day basis. He is usually from the area, while the politician is an import and less trusted by the people. The dons act as middle-men and they have the money to distribute and they drive flashy cars and frequently have an entourage of beautiful young ladies and a throng of 'bodyguards'. He is not seen very often in public but will be found at the big dancehall sessions in a private booth drinking the most expensive champagne and Hennessey, 'splashing' over his followers all night long.

Police Force

In the last five years or so, the government has toyed with the police force to find the right formula. They have imported Scotland Yard detectives, but the murder rate continues upward of fifteen hundred per year and the cleared up rate has declined from thirty five percent to twenty six percent. The statistics are considered to be conservative. The police force is not respected by the citizens because there is a perception, whether real or imagined, that the police force is a corrupt rogue body. The citizens refuse to share information with the police because they fear that the information would get back to the criminals and they would be killed. The killing of witnesses to crimes, have occurred on many occasions, which has justified the fear of the people.

The Jamaica Constabulary Force was born out of the 1865 Morant Bay Rebellion, when the force was formed to put down the uprising. It has been an adversarial relationship since. Many people in the society view the police force as oppressors and many members of the force deem the citizens as their enemies. The Suppression of Crimes Act, implemented during the Manley era and continued throughout Seaga's leadership, caused deterioration in the relationship between the citizens and the police. There were frequent instances where the police abused their powers and arrested people for days without bringing them to trial. Police patrols would go into communities and beat up the youths without them having any recourse to justice.

The police on the other hand, distrust the citizens because they would cover up for criminals in their communities. There are occasions when criminals engage the police in shootouts and the police end up killing these criminals, only to see the people mount demonstrations, as instructed by the dons and claim that the youths were killed innocently. This situation has been going on for years and the only respite came when Colonel Trevor McMillan was given the post of Police Commissioner during PJ Patterson's leadership but was rescinded a few years later because of differences with the government over a so-called 'contractual agreement'. The people's hopes were dashed for a truly professional police force.

Corruption

The plague of corruption runs rampant throughout Jamaica. In order to get the most basic thing done in a government department will require a payoff of cash or kind. You can be punished with undue delays if you don't grease somebody's palm. Transparency International has warned that Jamaica is close to 'state capture'. Corruption runs at all levels. Things are made artificially difficult to be accomplished and only those who can wait out the system or have money to pay their way to get it done quickly will accomplish anything. Party adherents will get things through their 'planted' public officials. Election financiers call in their chips as soon as the elections are over and board appointments are made to those who contributed. Whoever is known to the party hierarchy and that is so whether or not the individuals are qualified.

In order to get a driver's license you are expected to pay. You will not pass the test on your first or second tries. Many persons just prefer to buy the license rather than go through the inconvenience or the indignity of failing. Many things are done according to who you know or whichever of your friends know someone else.

The customs department, up until recently, had been a hotbed of corruption. Many officials in the department lived visibly way above their levels of remuneration. There would always be someone who acted on behalf of the official and that person was responsible for doing the collection. The money was then shared up among the parties involved.

The corruption at the customs department was a creation of government policies. A friend of mine, Byron Kerr, said that Jamaica is operated on bad mindedness and life must be made difficult for the Jamaican people. He wondered why people have to pay up to three hundred percent import duty on certain types of motor vehicles. He is of the opinion that people are motivated to work hard when they know that they can accomplish whatever their wants or needs are. Why would a government want to penalize someone because he desires a Lamborghini? The government's rationale is that certain types of expensive cars drain the country of valuable foreign exchange. What is that to the government? That is the car that I want and I agree with my friend that it is tantamount to bad mindedness to try and prevent me from owning what I worked hard for.

Government ministers and their cohorts, however, can import vehicles using a concession system that gives themselves waivers that the ordinary person cannot obtain. Whenever the duty is added to the cost, it makes it prohibitive for most of the population. People have sought every possible means to defeat that abusive system.

Some persons, who occupy high positions in the society, claim that too many cars are on the road and that the government should put a ban on car importation. The irony though, is that those people have three to four cars parked in their garages. All their kids drive to school and the stay at home wife also drives to the gym and the supermarket. Their errands and jobs are worthwhile to go to, but the common ordinary people should wait at the bus stops.

This is an elitist society with the plantocracy deeply entrenched and raging. We have gained independence as a country, but the vast majority of the people are dependent on a few with the wealth and power. Slavery has been abolished but the people are still enslaved. The rich and

powerful have captured the minds of the people and many of those who should have been educated are brain dead and have been fed a diet of brainwashed education. They toe the line of the masters and dare not put forward any independent thought and vision. A cursory glance at the masters will reveal that as a people we have not developed. The dark skinned people are still at the back. This picture is wrong and the people will find it out at some point. We should not wait until people's passions are inflamed. The time is now and the people want their seat at the table. If it's not given freely, then they may take it forcibly and that may be a disaster.

Migration

The Jamaican people have been leaving our shores for many years to live and work in other countries where they sense that there are better opportunities. Whether it was going to the motherland, England, or to help to build the Panama Canal, to work in Guantanamo Bay, to be a part of the Industrial Revolution in the United States or the farms of Canada. Jamaicans are always on the move and today, there are more Jamaicans living in other countries than the three million living in Jamaica.

The migratory tendencies of our people have fractured many families and the 'barrel-kids'; those children left behind by their parents to go search for a better life and send barrels of food and clothes to compensate for their absence; have been scarred and many are aimlessly, missing the love and warmth of their parents. Many of the boys especially, live wayward lives and grandparents have done the best they could.

Some studies have shown that the absence of some parents have caused children to end up in a life of crime. Yet there are government ministers, such as Perneal Charles, who are unable to fix our economy and provide for its people, have indicated that they are training people for export. The government relies on the people to get remittance money from their relatives abroad to keep them quiet. It has not dawned on the politicians that if our citizens make fifty thousand dollars in the United States and they had the right economic environment in Jamaica, they could be doing the same here, instead they will just settle with the five thousand that will be sent back home.

Even with people making such sacrifices, they are being ripped off by the system set up. The government has

HELL IN PARADISE

barred the citizens from receiving their remittances in the currency that was sent to them, instead there has been collusion with the conglomerates to pay the people in Jamaican dollars at rates that are lower than what their selling rates are. Maybe the people could go out into the marketplace, in the true spirit of a free-market system and obtain a higher or lower rate for their money.

The political and economic situation need to be cleaned up here, so that our countrymen will come back home to a peaceful and vibrant society, ready to compete with the rest of the world with the true indomitable spirit that has been displayed to the world via our track and field stars in the Beijing Olympics and the World Championships games in Germany. Jamaicans are tough and hardworking people, but the system has been crafted to stymie their abilities and their entrepreneurial spirit.

The vast majority of Jamaicans could be like the Matalon's, the Issa's, Mahfood's or the Ashenheim's. What the people need is the same access to capital and land. When you present a business plan to the bank and it is identical to the one presented by one of the well known families, I am inclined to believe that they will be more likely to secure a loan, than an ordinary Jamaican. On this point it may be necessary for the government to pass laws that bar discrimination in these instances. The banks should be made to retain the business plans presented to them and have the Bank of Jamaica or some other regulatory agency make frequent audits to determine if our suspicions are correct.

The Intellectual Ghetto

The number one talk-show host in the country Wilmot 'Mutty' Perkins coined the term 'intellectual ghetto' to describe the University of the West Indies. I suspect that he used ghetto to describe an urban sprawl that was unorganized and rarely produced anything positive.

He came up with this term because many of the people who have run government both at the political level and civil servants have graduated from that institution. If one takes a close look at the situation in Jamaica, it would not be difficult to agree with Mutty's analysis. The society has been decaying steadily for the last forty seven years and these lettered people have not been able to find a positive solution. The civil servants are hell-bent on preserving the legacy of colonialism. The school system has Britain written all over it and the writings and teachings of Marcus Garvey cannot find any place inside that elitism.

There is no room for people to be recognized on a first name basis; it is all about mister something or misses whatever. Every person who sits behind a desk wants to wield his or her power; that is even when no power comes with the job. It seems their ultimate purpose is to make life difficult for the common man and to massage the ego of anyone who seems 'up-townish', again, that is especially if that person is light-skinned and talks with an uptown accent. The system is so phony it makes you cringe.

The politicians are so eager to be in the company of the phony people's cocktail party that they will do nothing to change the status quo. They will party with them all night dancing calypso and the music at ear-busting decibel levels, but whenever they go to functions of their ordinary constituents, they will quickly disappear. They then go off

to pass night- noise laws that only apply to the poorer people in their constituencies.

Much of this sordid behavior emanates directly out of the intellectual ghetto. To possess a university degree from UWI makes the participants believe that they have some superior knowledge over other institutions; including the University of Technology and Northern Caribbean University, two very outstanding institutions. They demand more remuneration and their ultimate goal is to have a household helper and a gardener. Those achievements will give them the feeling that they have arrived and they will do everything in their powers to keep those persons right where they are.

In the workplace these 'bright' people will not buck the system. They quickly find out that their advancement is contingent on them sucking up to those people in positions above them and to beg and beseech the clerk's favors of what is rightfully their jobs. Many of these intellectually ghettoized people cannot make decisions and they bring nothing new to the table. They are bankrupt of ideas and hide behind their desks. If they are tackled about a situation, their answer is "that's the company policy or that is government's policy."

With so much decay around us, you would think that the intellectual ghetto would quickly come up with solutions. The Social Sciences Department is one of the largest on campus and yet there is just so much squalor in the society. They ought to take their classes out into the ghettos and get some hands on training. With that, Mutty may start believing in them.

Bruce Golding and the NDM

Bruce Golding has been a bright and articulate figure in the politics of Jamaica for a very long time. His becoming Prime Minister with the JLP has not been as significant as when he left the JLP and went on to form the National Democratic Movement.

Bruce was Chairman of the JLP when the 'gang of eleven' made up several MP's and other party officials from the West approached Golding and told him to approach Seaga to set in motion a timetable for his departure from leadership of the party. The party had lost the 89 and 93 general elections under Seaga's leadership and most of the members felt that he had become unelectable.

Seaga was in no mood for that message and many of Seaga's loyalists felt that Bruce was giving strength to the breakaway faction, which wanted Golding as leader.

Seaga shrewdly called for a leadership contest outside of their annual conference and set a margin below which he would not accept the leadership of the party. The Cuban-like election was held with Seaga being the only candidate and he was able to win with a comfortable margin above what he had set. In true Seaga style "argument done". He proclaimed that the delegates had spoken and that he would entertain no dissension in the party about his leadership, and to many others, on any other topic. He was seen as a dictator.

Bruce's popularity was rising among the electorate and inside the party. Seaga saw him as a definite threat and attempted to kill him politically. He publicly lambasted him and said that he did not have the balls for leadership and that he, Seaga, was the only one capable of running the party.

That public pronouncement crushed Golding's ego and he took a back seat from the JLP and took what he called an 'assessment of his continuation in politics'. He was seen as the natural leader for the Western dissidents and he went around the country getting a feel of the pulse of the people. All polls had shown that Jamaica was ready for a third party and those same polls saw Golding as the leader of a massive block of disenchanted voters.

His road trip became pivotal to his decision and he announced his resignation from the JLP and his intention to form a new political movement. His announcement from his party office in Munamar Square in Spanish Town reverberated around the entire country and as I write I still feel the goose pimples that I felt in 1995. The nation was on his back and the people felt like there was finally going to be a change in their lives from the squalor and criminality that pervaded our politics and which Golding spoke so eloquently about. Not since Michael Manley's 1972 leadership of the country, had the people felt so hopeful. I talked with old people in the rural areas and they were able to quickly indicate their willingness to vote for a third party for the first time in their lives.

Bruce went on to launch the National Democratic Movement at a massive function at the Jamaica Conference Centre in Downtown Kingston and had the PNP and JLP quaking in their boots. The political landscape had suddenly shifted and two old nemeses were searching for answers.

Stalwarts from the JLP and PNP quickly became members of the Movement and the new entity seemed like it was around for a long time and the brand NDM was quickly etched in the psyche of the Jamaican people here and in the Diaspora. Bruce Golding had pulled off a coup and it was now time for the hard work.

The PNP and JLP, without hesitation, locked horns and designed ways to kill the threat. Seaga quickly branded it the Benz and Bimmer party- indicating the middle-class nature of its following. Nothing was done by the new founder to counter that perception.

The party had cut across race, class, and political barriers and looked to be very promising. There was no shortage of money and well known personalities and political figures to take the movement to the top, or so we thought.

This new party had all the big names, the pedigree of its leadership was not in question and all that was left was for the party to romp to victory. It suddenly became a media darling and its message of 'new and different' resonated with the populace.

Soon after its launch there was an absence from the airwaves and the country was wondering why? The official word was that the party was behind the scenes preparing its policy positions. That was proved to be a terrible mistake.

Its absence gave the old parties enough time to calculate the threat and come up with a response. Their goal was to define the new movement and to put the leader who they always knew was vulnerable, on the defensive. They came up with terms such as 'a leopard cannot change its spot', which referred to Golding's admitted involvement in the corrosive politics in the country. They also called it the 'Brown man's party' which referred to the main composition of its leadership. It seems that by some 'accident' many in the leadership were light-skinned.

The PR machine that galvanized the movement seemed to be fizzling quickly and Bruce Golding, its leader,

seemed unprepared or possibly reluctant to mobilize the party into a cohesive and potent force to assume the leadership of the country.

In his own constituency of Central St Catherine he had solid support among his constituents. His was a garrison constituency and he was responsible for making it so. With his breakaway from the JLP, they felt that they had to dislodge him and prevent the NDM from winning the seat. They sent his brother-in-law Perneal Charles to wrest control but he found the going tough and ran east. The JLP then decided that Karl Samuda, a turncoat that went to the PNP and ran back to the JLP when things did not go his way should try his luck. Things also seemed not to be in his favor and he ran as well. The consensus was that someone had to go in there and be prepared to deal with the rough and tumble to dislodge Golding. The JLP turned to Babsy Grange and she seemed to be the perfect fit.

She was heavily schooled into organizing garrison politics and she did not disappoint. The dons who once supported Golding as well as the new emerging One Order gang, were brought into the fold and reminded that they were Labourites first and Golding supporters second. They were ordered to fall in line behind the party and the 'mother of all garrisons' played a role into settling the issue.

Bruce Golding was already branded as master planner of the JLP's enforcement arm in the 1980 election and his own admission that he knew about violence perpetrated against the PNP, placed him in a box. His every movement was watched and he had declared that he was 'new and different' and that the NDM of which he was leader would not be involved in any violence.

He literally gave up his constituency without a fight. His support was strong enough to win the constituency if he had engaged with the people from door to door. He however, preferred to campaign on the television and that weakened his support on the ground. It was felt that had he gone in on the ground, it would have been a bloody fight between himself and Babsy Grange. Other observers thought that the media spotlight would have been bright in the constituency and would have prevented Grange from carrying on any hanky panky. He barely kept any meetings and many of the constituents started feeling that he was not serious and went with the JLP instead.

His 'new and different' philosophy meant that there would no longer be any issuing of guns or for there to be any violence in elections and the buying of votes would not be entertained. It also included, not buying any curry goat and white rum for the usual festivities. Many of the supporters had gotten used to those things being offered and therefore, they would not support anyone who would deprive them of their 'windfall' garnered every five years.

The general election was held in 1998 and Bruce lost to Babsy. It seemed that shortly after the NDM was formed Bruce became lonely in his new party and was hell-bent on returning to the JLP. That theory was put forward by a legal luminary in his party Dr Stephen Vascianne. Bruce denied it on many occasions, but he constantly acted like a prodigal son and seemed desperate to return to the fold of the JLP.

He would find all the adjectives in the world to describe the PNP but he was always without words that he felt would hurt the JLP. The Jamaican people started branding the NDM as 'the baby JLP'. He did nothing to shake that stigma and with the NDM failing to win any seat in the 98

election, Bruce appeared to be looking for the quickest exit he could find.

There was a by-election in 2001 in the North-East St Ann constituency and the NDM nominated a formidable candidate in Barbara Clarke. The NDM felt confident that they could win the by-election and restore some confidence in the prospect of the NDM. The party was mobilized and very often Bruce would appear like a reluctant warrior and his party members seemed to be always pulling him into directions that he was afraid to go or in areas where he did not want to upset his former party.

After the NDM only got seven percent of the votes in that constituency, which the JLP won, upsetting the ruling PNP, which held the seat for many years, the opportunity presented itself for Golding to lap his tail and run away from the leadership of the brightest prospect for Jamaica to change its dirty politics. He wasted no time and within days at Dinthill Technical High School in Linstead St. Catherine he announced his resignation from the party, which only a few years before he had co-founded.

After his departure the NDM grappled to hold on in the dark. Many of its most prominent figures departed with him and left the NDM to die.

In my opinion the failure of the NDM to not win a seat in parliament or not to win State power, was the most gigantic failure of leadership ever witnessed in Jamaica and possibly the entire Caribbean. Never before in this region were so many people of quality assembled under one umbrella. Never before have so many people from academia come together to support a party and never before has businesses and the moneyed class given so generously to a political party. The way Bruce Golding screwed up the most viable third party ever formed in Jamaica, will have to be analyzed for generations to come. The death of the NDM caused Jamaicans to lose hope again and continues to be reflected in the low voter turnout in General Elections.

Renato Adams

Renato Valentino Decordova Adams has been one of the most colorful figures to have appeared on the Jamaican scene in many years. Not since the likes of Bob Marley and Jimmy Cliff in his role in the movie, "The Harder They Come", has someone so skillfully captured the hearts and minds of Jamaicans. He recited his entire name on a call to Mutty Perkins and Mutty repeated it daily on his call-in program until it became familiar to Jamaicans.

Renato Adams was a member of the Jamaica Constabulary Force for about forty years but became prominent in the last ten years. Crime has always been a problem in Jamaica and the Jamaican people would always want to find crime-fighters from the police force, who they thought, stood between themselves and the criminals. Many persons have occupied those positions from time to time. The likes of; Joe Williams, Bigga Ford, Laing, Tony Hewitt, Karate Georgie in Montego Bay, Bag-an-Pan in St Elizabeth, Harry Bungles, Hux, Kelso Small, and Trinity, just to name of few.

Those members of the force gave the citizens some level of confidence that we could get rid of the gunmen. Many of them would figure very prominently in high profile shootouts or 'alleged' shootouts with gunmen and that would usually make them famous. In the case of Karate Georgie, he would take on criminals in Montego Bay and as a martial arts fighter; he would duel with pickpockets and others who were brazen to fight the police in public, which has become a common phenomenon.

Renato Adams almost sudden appearance on the crime fighting scene started in the 90s when the PNP seemed unable to find any solutions to the rising crime despite its National Security Minister K.D. Knight boasting about the number of pieces of legislation that he had brought to parliament.

Like other governments before it, the PJ Patterson government responded to the rising crime with the formation of 'special' police squads. The murder rate had moved up from four hundred per year to six hundred within two years of the formation of the government and among the victims were a couple of high profile names. The government's response was A.C.I.D. or the Anti Crime Investigative Detachment.

There were howls of protest against the acronym by human rights groups because acid is a corrosive substance that was regularly used in street fights in Jamaica to maim and disfigure ones opponent. The government relented and changed the name to the Special Anti Crime Task Force. Renato Adams was selected to become a part of this unit.

It was close to the time that Jamaica's newest television station, CVM was formed and the station was hungry for news. It had to find a way to win the minds of Jamaicans who had gotten used to their only TV station since independence, the JBC. Milton Walker and Michael Pryce found a very close ally in Renato Adams and for the first time the Jamaican public had live police operations taking place in their living rooms via CVM. Renato Adams was the star and the public loved him. His every move was followed and it was clear that he was enjoying his role. He was transferred to Spanish Town, another hotbed of criminality and the TV cameras followed him. He began his sojourn there by removing the vendors off the streets and this was welcomed by the residents of Spanish Town, who were jostling with vendors for the walkways. He was always hands on and unlike many police Superintendents; he would be heavily involved in the frontline of operations in his division. He was always able to put the spin on things that would play out well on television. Michael Pryce and Milton Walker were not going to report anything that would jeopardize their 'privileged' position in Adam's operations.

Whenever any shootings or killings took place in Adams' division involving the police he would quickly place himself on the scene and was able to give a full account of the events and again CVM would be his messenger. Many persons in the society ate his every word and would take his account, as gospel. He had built up trust with a vast majority of the Jamaican people and the human rights lobby, who tried to take the shine off his ball, was roundly condemned by Jamaicans at home and abroad.

He won many praises for his management of crime in Spanish Town, despite the fact that he failed to dismantle the two main gangs operating in the town, The Klansman and One Order Gangs. His PR was more powerful than his performance and he was rewarded with a transfer to another new 'special squad' The Crime Management Unit.

The murder rate had now climbed to eight hundred and again a few high profile names were among the victims. This is usually the only time that the political directorate will be spurred into action. Adams was given the mandate and the resources to root out criminals in all parts of the country. It was promised that the unit would be intelligence driven. He was able to handpick its members and it was reported that the usual chain of command was bypassed and he reported directly to the Prime Minister.

Jamaicans celebrated but the human rights groups were not amused. They thought that Adams was responsible for extra-judicial killings and they raised their objections. Adams was such a master of public relations, he was able to turn the spotlight on his adversaries and they were the ones who earned the wrath of Jamaicans. Adams was able to capitalize on the fear of the people and made himself the David facing the criminals, Goliath.

His management of the CMU was very controversial. In the eyes of the vast majority he was doing a great job of killing the murderers, while the human rights group continued to be a thorn in his flesh. He was charged for the murder in an operation in Clarendon when he reportedly went in search of "Chen Chen", a man wanted for murder. The wanted man escaped but in an alleged shootout one woman was killed along with another man.

The human rights group, Jamaicans for Justice led by the tenacious Dr Carolyn Gomes demanded a thorough investigation into the incident and Scotland Yard detectives led by Mark Shields was called in to spearhead the investigation. While this investigation was taking place Adams was involved in another highly controversial shooting incident in Portmore St Catherine, which became known as the 'Braeton 7', in that incident seven young men, none older than 19, were killed in a house in what Adams alleged was a shootout.

It was claimed that acting on intelligence the police had gone to the location in search of wanted men who were involved in the murder of a school principal. Adams reported that on arrival at the location they were greeted with gunfire from the house in which the men were located. He said the police returned the fire and the men were later found suffering from gunshot wounds and were

taken to hospital where they were pronounced dead. That piece was very commonly used when the police are involved in fatal shootings.

Adams seemed to flourish under these controversies and his popularity rose higher. The majority of Jamaicans wanted him to become the police commissioner whenever the position became vacant but the government wilted under the pressure of Jamaicans for Justice, who aligned themselves with International Human Rights organizations such as Amnesty International which thwarted any such intentions. Adams' visa to the United States and the United Kingdom were cancelled by those countries.

He was acquitted of the murder charge and returned to the force. Again Carolyn Gomes proved very effective by putting pressure on the government and he was placed at a desk job with very little responsibility. He remained popular with the Jamaican people and his PR machine remains relevant. He was not afraid to tackle any issue or answer any questions that were asked of him. He answered questions in a refreshing way, which endeared him to the populace. He attacked the corruption in the police force, which was known in the wider society but was never attacked from within with the ferocity with which Adams did. He would criticize politicians, another area that other members of the force would refrain.

Adams earned his reputation in a big way in the Tivoli Gardens Massacre when in the lead up to the 2003 general election he carried out an operation in Tivoli Gardens in which twenty one people were killed. Many persons including the

Member of Parliament for the area thought that it was politically motivated.

There was a common pattern over the years to demonize Edward Seaga and his association with the 'mother of all garrisons', Tivoli Gardens. When leading up to an election with the PNP as government something usually happen, in this case Adams and a police party were assembling in the vicinity of the Denham Town Police Station and were reportedly fired on by men from the adjoining high rise buildings in Tivoli. A three days shootout ensued and at the end twenty one citizens were killed in the streets. A Commission of Enquiry was held but no one was found criminally responsible.

The prior election saw the police finding a large quantity of ammunition in the community of Tivoli and police uniforms, reportedly being prepared to use on Election Day. A man was reportedly charged but the public was never told of the outcome of that case. In another incident in Tivoli Gardens a few years prior, the police commissioner intimated that there were underground tunnels in the community, which allowed criminals to easily escape from the police. There has not been any proof presented about the tunnels. In another incident the police claimed that they had found evidence in the community that there was a court system set up internally which tried people and 'convicted' them and there was an execution chamber in which killings took place execution style.

These stories among others remained vivid in the mind of the populace and Adams did not have a problem selling the Tivoli operation to us. Edward Seaga as usual, stoutly defended his constituents and again he was marked down by the electorate. If the position of police commissioner was decided by an election; Adams would have won hands down. His rhetoric however, had more bark than bite. While he was at the CMU the murder rate in the country

had moved from eight hundred to sixteen hundred when he left. The public would not notice that statistic and would probably flatly deny it. Adams' popularity will remain until the murder rate falls precipitously.

Custom's Department

The custom's department up until recently was the seat of corruption in Jamaica. It was rescued by Danville Walker, a no-nonsense former Jamaica Defense Force Officer who returned to the island after migrating to the United States. His first job on his return to Jamaica was to head the contentious position of Director of Elections. It was a post that has broken the heart of many persons who have served faithfully but was always blamed by the losing party as its failure for not winning elections.

Danville brought a firm hand to the position and he did not allow the politicians to push him around. He was constantly on the public airwaves bringing clarity to any misinformation put out by the politicians. His conduct of elections were considered fair and he was respected by both the PNP and JLP.

On his assumption of the leadership of the customs department, he quickly started to shuffle the deck and had customs officers hopping mad about his leadership. He reminded people of the way Colonel Trevor McMillan shook up the police force when he was appointed Commissioner of Police. Walker's job was to cut out corruption and to make the department more efficient and to safeguard government revenue. He has created a better image for customs, but the persons who were rooted in the corruption are not finding the going as prosperous as they used to.

The tariffs charged by the government on many imported items are downright oppressive and gives rise to many persons to try to beat the system. Take for example, the importation duty on motor vehicles. In some instances, you will be charged up to three hundred percent duty on a car depending on the size of the car's engine. Imagine yourself paying for a car four times to get it into the country. It is done according to the authorities, to prevent people from using valuable foreign exchange for buying cars. Yet they waste more money buying second hand cars from Japan and have to spend enormous sums buying spare parts. Talk about being penny wise and pound foolish.

The politicians have however, insulated themselves from their own draconian impositions. They have allowed themselves to pay only twenty percent tariff on the cars that they import. They have also sided with senior civil servants for them to pay a similar amount. When there is an election, the parties are allowed to import cars duty free for election campaigns. Many of the titans of the private sector get around the high tariffs for motor vehicles by serving on the boards of statutory bodies and other government departments.

What is the motivation for people to work hard and to buy the things that they desire? Most people shy away from buying a Benz or a BMW because they would not be able to afford the cost of clearing it from the wharves. This has forced many persons to migrate, in order that they can have the freedom to buy what they want without any hindrance. This is a disincentive to young qualified persons to remain in the country, but the status quo must remain at all cost and that is one way of ensuring that it does.

Interest Groups

The Jamaican society is controlled by a few interest groups, mainly the Private Sector Organization of Jamaica (PSOJ), The Jamaica Chamber of Commerce (JCC) and the Jamaica Manufacturers Association (JMA). These people wield enormous influence, although their numbers are small. That power is derived from their abilities to fund the campaigns for elections and governments quake in their boots whenever any of these bodies come out with a statement against them. They are backed up by the media which in many instances are owned by individuals or groups that are also part of these organizations. And most importantly is that the skin tone of these persons will reveal once more that the majority of these persons are either light skinned or white. I guess it may just be by accident again?

Missed Opportunities

I harp on the color of the people who seem to perpetually run the show because they are a tiny minority and they are in control of about ninety five percent of the economy. It would be stupid for someone to think that this could happen, without it being designed that way. They have used all the systems that the former slave masters used to control the slaves, to maintain their dominance. They are not about to give up their right to have poor black Jamaican women struggle on a bus or by foot to get to their uptown mansions to be their nannies or their household helpers.

When they fled to Miami during Michael Manley's reign in the seventies, they had to do their own gardening and house work and they are hell bent on making sure that it never happens again. They are not going to lose the power of having their gardeners drive in the back seat while the front passenger seat is empty, to come to the town center to pick up every piece of item that they purchase, while they walk around empty-handed.

The power elite are making a grand mistake and are missing great opportunities to have even more wealth. If they encourage their verandah buddies (the politicians), to create more economic opportunities for the dispossessed, it is quite likely that they would become richer and there would be less crime. They should ensure that the politicians provide quality schools all around than the few KC's, JC's, Campion's, and Immaculate's but rather some better Donald Quarrie's, Norman Manley's,

Trench Town's and Charlie Smith's. That kind of thinking is not in their DNA and only when this powder keg explodes, will they realize the fallacy of their mission.

Air Jamaica

The National airline, Air Jamaica, has been a cherished asset of the Jamaican people, especially those in the Diaspora. Many Jamaicans will not be caught flying on any other airline. They would boast about the smooth landing of the Jamaican pilots and the native dishes that were served aboard the aircraft.

The airline has however, been a drain on the resources of the country. Its name and what it represents were the only assets. It cost the taxpayers millions in subsidies annually to keep it afloat. It was used by politicians and their families as a private family car. Its Chairman could turn back a flight to pick up a favored person who was late. The mismanagement of the carrier was glaring. The planes were often late and caused many passengers to be frustrated. The customer service was questionable and left a lot to be desired. The crux of the matter however, was that the people loved their Air Jamaica and did not have any desire to part with it.

So when the Jamaican government under Bruce Golding's leadership decided to sell the airline; there was mixed reaction among the population. Many persons felt that the government could not continue its ownership and that it should be divested; others felt that it should remain in the hands of the people via the government.

In the early 1990's it was divested to the Butch Stewart led Air Jamaica Acquisition Group but its financial position continued to deteriorate and though its on-time performance improved dramatically, its viability was precarious. The private owners purchased new aircrafts and added many non-profitable routes to its schedule. The airline was being used as a shuttle carrier to filter tourists into the hotels.

On the surface, that seems plausible, since Jamaica depends on tourism as one of its major sources of revenue. The problem though, was that Butch was a major player in the tourism industry and the fact that all the loans borrowed by this private company was guaranteed by the government and people of Jamaica. This was a clear conflict of interest, but the guarantees continued unabated. The airline was eventually turned back over to government with a huge debt.

A young parliamentarian, Andrew Gallimore raised the issue of the indebtedness of the airline in the people's parliament but was smacked down by his leader, Bruce Golding. Many moons have passed and still no clearer insight into how a private company was allowed to run up so much debt in the name of the country. The taxpayers have been left with the bag.

The airline is being divested again and there is a whole lot of controversy surrounded the process. It was first expected that it would have been taken over by Spirit Airlines but that deal fell through and it was then supposedly turned over the next higher bidder. That meant that the Trinidadian owned Caribbean Airlines was next in line to bid. This caused some consternation in both countries. The Trinidadians were not thrilled that their government was buying an airline that was bankrupt and would not add any value to Trinidad's national carrier. In Jamaica on the other hand, they did not like the idea that the Trinis were coming into their country and buying up all the prized properties. The Bruce Golding led government nonetheless continued to negotiate with Trinidad.

The passions were raised in Jamaica when some employees of Air Jamaica, who called themselves the Air Jamaica Pilots Association, but included other workers; placed a bid for the airline as well. This move seemed to have irritated the government and they tried to smack them down. At first the government refused to look at their bid, but with public pressure and smart public relations from the group, the government decided to take a look at their proposal.

The impression given by the government was that the group was an irritant and did not have the financial backing to take over the running of an airline. The government had their own timeline to sell the airline and with a pending agreement with the International Monetary Fund (IMF), which dictated that it be sold, there was no inclination to deal with any other bid.

With the government's unwillingness to entertain any other bid, the Trinidadians felt comfortable to dictate the negotiations. It seemed that they were constantly moving the goalpost and wanted to only buy the profitable routes. They would not assume any of the airline's debt and wanted Caribbean Airlines to be the national carrier for Jamaica.

The Jamaican public was bewildered by Caribbean Airline's posture. The majority of the people thought that if we were going to give away the airline, we should give it away to the Jamaican entity that showed interest.

A friend of mine Peter Townsend put it succinctly. He said that if he had a motorcycle to sell and a friend came to him to buy it and his son made the same offer. He would have no choice but to sell it to his son. That is the scenario that existed with the Air Jamaica divestment and it is still pending or it will fold if the parties cannot agree to the terms.

Re-Awakening the People

Is there hope for Jamaica? That's a question that occupies my mind on a daily basis. Whenever I look at the political leadership from the PNP and the JLP, I become despondent. There are no big thinkers on the horizon in any of those two entities, and being the parties that the Jamaican people have their umbilical cords tied to, it seems like a hopeless situation.

The Jamaican people will have to look towards some new younger leaders who are detached from the thinking of our old political culture. Those new young bloods will have to be able to unite the people and dismantle the corrosive system that has been so solidly built up by the criminal organizations; the People's National Party and the Jamaica Labour Party.

There can be no dispute that these two bodies plotted and organized the garrisons and in the early days supplied the enforcers with the weaponry used to kill and maim people from other communities and also force the inhabitants of its own neighborhoods to conform to the dictates of dons. The two parties have presided over a system that has created the dubious distinction of having the country ranking as the most murderous in the world. The PNP and JLP have forced many of our citizens to be 'refugees' in other countries, having to flee from the war zone that Jamaica has become.

These two parties that have guided them through independence should not be upset of my characterization of them. They need to explain the underdevelopment of our nation. They need to justify why many of our schools are still using pit latrines. They should explain their inability to build dams to adequately provide such a basic commodity as water for its citizens. They need to explain the poor management of the economy and the dismal performance of our currency. They should justify to the country that it was worth us gaining independence from Britain.

Our young people will have to muster all their natural talents and abilities and almost completely disregard practices of their parents and make a clean break with the past. They will have to chart a course that will inspire the next generation to achieve the greatness that comes natural to us, but has been stymied by our useless leaders. It is said that the people get the leaders that they deserve but our leaders have been foisted upon us.

Coalition Government

Bruce Golding took over the reigns' of the government in September of 2007 and had the entire nation hoping for some real positive changes. They have instead given the impression that they had no preparation, although they were in opposition for eighteen years. They came out of the starting blocks falling on their faces and have been floating around like a big rudderless ship. They are out of their depths and need to be rescued. It seems that we are unable to get any new blood or new thinking into the existing political structure in the near future and we therefore have to find some alternatives as a stop gap measure.

I think that we should seriously consider suspending our constitution and have some kind of power sharing arrangement set up in the Parliament and a Cabinet comprising the present prime minister retaining his position for two more years and the Opposition Leader becoming the deputy prime minister.

There should be an equal number of Cabinet ministers serving on both sides of the political divide. The roles of the prime minister and the deputy prime minister will be reversed after Golding's next two years and Portia Simpson will become prime minister, but the roles of the ministers would remain the same. Non-performing ministers would be replaced with someone from the same party.

There would be no election in the next eight years and the constituency representation would remain the same. If the MP is older than 70, he should relinquish his/her position as MP and, with the consultation of the party, he/she would appoint a suitable successor from the party. That age barrier should not preclude those MP's from serving as ministers of government.

We should recognize that the political parties have only slight ideological differences and so there has to be a mechanism worked out to settle those differences at the Cabinet level. We should appoint an arbitration panel headed by the Governor General and the local Privy Council, as well as members of the Electoral Commission to be final arbiters on any major ideological differences that may arise in the Cabinet.

What the country needs at the moment is some breathing room, so that we can extricate ourselves from the corrosive politics that has so engulfed us over the last forty years. If we could pull this off we could then tackle some very big issues such as crime, the economy and our badly run-down social services in a bi-partisan or non-partisan manner.

Dismantling the Garrisons

Any change in our circumstances will only be achieved if we decide to systematically dismantle the garrisons. Many of these garrisons occupy prime real estate in Kingston and Montego Bay. We will have to find a way to build housing in the rural areas for these people and move them out of the cities back to the rural areas from which they originated. We must provide housing and jobs for them and free up the spaces in the cities for major developments of shopping malls and commercial enterprises. This is a special situation where gentrification should be accommodated. Too many unplanned and squalid conditions exist in these areas.

With eighty percent of all major crimes emanating from these garrisons, it stands to reason that if they are dismantled and the people scattered all over the place and the proper police intelligence system is instituted to prevent them from regrouping in their present form, we would see a precipitous fall in crime.

With a lower crime rate, Jamaicans would be returning home in droves to set up businesses. The tourism industry would boom and other private overseas investors would find Jamaica an attractive investment destination. The desire to have an offshore financial center would become so much more attractive. Health tourism in a relaxed and crime-free environment would be a dream come true and major conferences would not want to pass up Jamaica as a preferred choice.

There is so much that we have. The country is so beautiful; the vibes of the Jamaican people can be so friendly and electrifying. It is just puzzling; why are we failing as nation? It pains my heart that the government has the answer but because of selfish reasons, refuses to get the right people in place to run the various institutions. The PNP and JLP prefers to staff the public bodies with persons who contributed to their campaigns and their political lackeys, rather than the most qualified people. The political parties have instituted policies to continue to oppress the people, rather than release their innate talents and entrepreneurial spirits.

The government refuses to listen to the suggestions of its citizens and believe that they have a monopoly on ideas. They are content with using the old washed-over ideas that have failed dramatically. The status quo is benefiting a few, and those are the ones who are listened to. They are the people who can invite the politicians to sit on their verandahs and enjoy the finest liquors.

Gun Ownership

It is quite alarming the rising murder rate that the country has been experiencing over the last 20 years. Governments over this period have given very little assurance to the population that they know how to tackle the problem. Despite their best intentions and the numerous high-level police units put in place (Operation Ardent, Eradication Squad, ACID-later Special Anti Crime Task Force and many others), we have not had many successes.

We have moved from 400 murders in 1989 to over 1,600 in 2007 and exceeded that number in 2008 and 2009. In the first four months of 2010, the country recorded over 600 murders and was on track to break all records in that category of crime statistics. These are staggering numbers. Most of these murders are committed by a few brazen gunmen, who are well armed and who go about their business killing and maiming law-abiding citizens with impunity. They know that less than 30 percent of the murders are solved and therefore there is no fear that they will be caught. We constantly repeat the same washed-over ideas when there is a spike in murders or when some 'big-named' person is killed.

It is time to take a different approach. This is an emergency situation and the government needs to deal with the crime problem as if it were a national crisis and treat it as such. The entire country needs to be mobilized around this cause. We need to recognize that the lawless elements in our society go to any extreme to gain access to guns (whether from Haiti, in barrels from the U.S or from Colombia). These guns have made them extremely powerful and have put them in a complete advantageous position over the law-abiding citizens.

The restrictions and bureaucracy put in place by the previous firearm law and now the Firearm Licensing Authority, for obtaining a licensed firearm is a slap in the face of law-abiding citizens who have decided to play by the rules. In taking back our communities we need to arm our citizens who:

1. Are at least 21 years old
2. Have no criminal record
3. Have no mental problems
4. Show the competence to handle a firearm

This is not a wild-west proposal. We have to be practical and realize that criminals have no fear and it is time to take the fight right back to them. If a criminal decides that he is going into a community and kick in a door, he should face a barrage of community shotguns. If a few gunmen decide that they are going to hold up a bus and they think that the passengers are armed, it is less likely that they will go rob the buses. Similarly, the brazen gunman who went into the middle of Half-Way-Tree and killed that hairdresser, thought about the risk and easily realized that it was very unlikely that he would have been challenged by hundreds of citizens in the area, who were more likely to be unarmed. He was able to carry out his deadly mission unperturbed. It is time to level the playing field.

I had my personal experience on February 7, 2010 in Spanish Town when a lone gunman hid in the cab of a trailer. I had been doing some work on a property that I own. I had just managed to get a glimpse of him when he popped his head up inside the cab. For a moment, I thought it might have been the driver and so, I looked in the direction of where the driver was on the property and realized that it

HELL IN PARADISE

was a stranger. By the time I looked back at the trailer, the gunman jumped out and started blazing shots at me. I immediately threw myself to the ground, as I was taught by instructors in the Jamaica Constabulary Force, the United States Navy and my current trainer Captain 'Kappo' Hibbert. While on my way to the ground I pulled my firearm and fired back in the gunman's direction. He ran behind a tree and used it as cover. I was in the open and was able to roll several times to make myself a moving target. I managed to scare the gunman from behind the tree and then took it as my cover. It was the nearest hard object close to me. He then managed to run behind a sand mound and evaded my bullets and then he got behind a tree. All this time, he was firing shots from his 9mm pistol as if he had broken into an armory. He realized at one point when my gun was jammed that there was an opportunity to come close and he came within twenty feet of me. I was just able to eject the bad bullet from my gun and re-inserted my magazine and slide it forward. He was almost on top of me and I was able to quickly get off three rounds into his chest and it was at this point that I realized that he had on a bulletproof vest. He staggered backwards and ran back behind the tree. He then ran behind another sand mound close to a river on the property and at that time I realized that I was shot in my knee. For a while I did not see him and did not hear him firing anymore shots and I managed to scramble towards the road to seek assistance to get to the hospital. Our shootout lasted for about fifteen minutes. My workers were there and saw the entire episode but could not help because they were not armed. The police recovered over thirty spent shells from the gunman's gun and fourteen from mine. He was well prepared and came for a battle. I still don't know what his motive was, but I am glad that I was armed or I would be a sitting duck and that would not be nice.

Some people theorize that he may have come for my firearm. That could be so, but I have seen gunmen go to kill people for their money and just about anything else. My firearm saved my life. My regret was that my workers were not armed, because we could have been a real challenge to that gunman and he may not have escaped.

More than ever before, I think that we need to arm our citizens. When I formed the National Gun Rights Association just over a year ago, it was in keeping with my belief that too many restrictions were in place to arm the ordinary citizens who were confronted by armed criminals on a daily basis and were helpless and in many instances were killed. There were also some who were armed and were still killed, but not nearly as many as who were unarmed.

On March 24, 2006, former JLP Senator Prudence Kidd-Deans, who I call the mother of the gun rights movement in Jamaica, argued in the Senate that all members of the public who qualified for firearm licenses, and who wanted and could afford the weapons, should have easier access to them. She also called for the removal of bureaucratic impediments to granting gun licenses. She was willing to take a guess that at least 75 percent of Jamaica's legislators on both sides of the political divide were licensed firearm holders, and she noted that those who qualified were provided with security personnel, in contrast with other Jamaicans who 'must abide by the rules of the State and at the same time tremble with fear at the possibility of the gunman's bullet'. Mrs. Kidd-Deans called for every level of bureaucracy to be removed to facilitate the application of every decent law-abiding Jamaican who has applied, and

who fit the criteria for a firearm license, and that such a person is granted one unhesitatingly and expeditiously so that a person can become a front-line soldier in his or her defense.

Colonel Trevor McMillan a former police commissioner, and who became the Minister of National Security when the NGRA was formed was asked about Kidd-Dean's proposal at the time it was made and he strongly supported it by saying, "Placing more guns in the hands of responsible citizens would deter crime." He was reported further in the Jamaica Observer newspaper as saying, "Think about it, haven't you heard of cases where armed citizens have intervened to stop a robbery or save someone's life? It can work." McMillan was against a civilian board as the best way to go about the issuing of licenses and feared that they might get bogged down in details. He questioned what objective rationale would be used to determine who got a license.

The Firearm License Authority, as predicted by McMillan is indeed bogged down in details, but the sad thing was that McMillan did nothing to change that when he was the National Security Minister and had portfolio responsibility for the agency. Members of our association were refused a license with the reason being, Applicant has not shown a need for a firearm. One classic refusal was Applicant is a Security guard, no need for a licensed firearm. What are the criteria used? How can someone who has met the essential requirement, be given such flimsy reason, in this country with the highest murder rate in the world? It is time to empower our citizens, whether they are from uptown or downtown, whether they carry around large sums of money or not. If we can't trust our law-abiding citizens to take care of themselves, then the worst is yet to come. We must make gunmanship a high-risk job so that it loses its glamour. The gunman must cringe in fear of attacking a citizen and not the other way around.

In the United States, crime is lower in the states that have more liberal gun policies such as Florida, Wyoming, Montana and Texas; on the other hand, the states which have restrictive gun laws, such as Chicago, Washington DC and New York have higher crime rates. In Europe, countries such as Switzerland and Finland are almost crime-free and are attributable to the very liberal gun laws and the training afforded to its law-abiding citizens.

The Government needs to think outside the box and listen to another of the mothers of the gun rights movement in the country. Sally Porteous, who was a victim of crime, made it known that she will not be caught off-guard again. We cannot fix our economy if we cannot fix the crime. The citizens will be ready if they are called to action and given the requisite training. It's time to trust our people and let them play their part. We cannot allow gun ownership to remain a commodity for the elite in the society. This apartheid system of gun ownership must go. Poor people are more vulnerable and need to protect their families as well. They too want to go bird shooting with their families as a sport. It is a crying shame to see this aspect of our colonial past so deeply entrenched.

Christopher 'Dudus' Coke

In August of 2009 the United States Government, by way a Grand Jury in New York, handed down an indictment for Christopher Coke alias 'presi', 'shortman' 'president' and 'dudus'. The indictment alleged that he was involved in drug exports to the United States and that he participated in interstate trading in illegal arms within the United States via telephone conversations. It was reported that he had never travelled to the United States.

Coke is the son of the former feared leader of West Kingston, Lester Lloyd Coke, alias Jim Brown, who was mentioned earlier. He was also wanted by the US but was mysteriously burnt up in his jail cell in the general Penetentiary, while he awaited extradition. The son, like father before him controlled the garrison community of West Kingston and in particular Tivoli Gardens, built and bred by Edward Seaga- the 'Father of all Garrisons'.

Tivoli Gardens has been known to be the bastion and headquarters of the international criminal organization known as the Shower Posse. This unit was formed in the 1980's by Jim Brown, Vivian Blake and 'Storyteller' Morrison. In its infancy, it wreaked havoc across the United States and Great Britain and controlled a great deal of the crack cocaine distribution in the East Coast/West Coast trade in narcotics; with major distribution hubs in California, Miami and New York.

Their notoriety was enhanced by the ruthless nature of their operations. Any betrayal was greeted with death and there was major gun running involved with their operations. It is believed that the word Shower, in Shower Posse came from the way the gunmen associated with the gang, were able to spray bullets on their opponents in the quantity and ferocity of a major downpour of rain.

Dudus inherited the leadership of the gang after his father was killed and his brother 'Jah T' was also murdered shortly afterwards on Maxfield Avenue in Kingston. He was known in the early days of his leadership to be brutal and inspired fear in his community. His name was turned over to the police commissioner Colonel Trevor McMillan by the Member of Parliament Edward Seaga among a list of thirteen persons in 1994, which Seaga alleged were terrorizing the community and should be arrested. McMillan rebuffed Seaga, acknowledging that he did not have any evidence to prosecute him.

It seems that Dudus matured in his role as leader of the powerful organization and ran Tivoli with an iron-fist. He facilitated 'law & order' in Tivoli and ensured that 'quick justice' was delivered in whatever form he thought appropriate, and his method gained the confidence and trust of his followers and the community. Dudus gained even more prominence by forming alliances with dons associated with the PNP such as Donald 'Zeeks' Phipps, of Matthews Lane in Downtown Kingston and Danhai Williams.

These alliances reduced the political tension and robustly ensured the easy facilitation and movement of drugs and guns in the criminal underworld. The dons were able to stretch their tentacles throughout the major ghettos in Jamaica. They were seen together at major reggae shows and dances covorting with each other. The famous Passa Passa dance held in West Kingston attracted uptown and downtown and gang leaders would not be left out.

They were prominent faces and some of Jamaica's most beautiful women and famous dancers would be on show. Dudus created this attraction and in the process attracted thousands of people on a Tuesday night, into daylight on Wednesday mornings. There have never been any reports of violence or car theft. With Dudus's leadership the crime rate in West Kingston police division, usually very high, went down significantly.

Dudus' underground empire seems to have amassed significant wealth and was evidenced by the latest BMW's in his entourage. His promotion company, Presidential Click, was the promoter of many stage shows. He is also a major shareholder in Incomparable Enterprise, which received millions of dollars in contracts from the Kingston and St Andrew Corporation, the local government body responsible for the Corporate Area. This body is led by the Mayor Desmond McKenzie, who is a product of Tivoli Gardens. The company is also the beneficiary of sub-contracts from reputable companies in receipt of government contracts. Incomparable Enterprise has received quarry licenses from the Bruce Golding led Urban Development Corporation, to supply millions of dollars worth of marl to construction projects and to provide other trucking services.

It is reported that Dudus is not one to delve too deeply into politics like his father was, but he understands the dynamics of the political situation in the country and the cover it provides for his activities. He therefore embraced the politicians that will benefit him and provide protection from incursion from the security forces into his fortified enclave. Having Prime Ministers representing his constituency is an ideal situation to be in.

The constituency was represented by Edward Seaga for forty years and during that time his father became a well-known don and contractor, especially during the eight years that Seaga ruled as Prime Minister 1980-1989. He remained Opposition Leader up until 2005 and thus occupied a powerful position in the constitutional arrangement in Jamaica.

Seaga was feared and with the political enclave of Tivoli that he built up, it was an unwritten rule that the police should not venture into the community without being invited in by the don. In 2001 under the PNP administration and what some people deemed to have been politically motivated, to demonize Seaga close to a general election. The fearless Renato Adams and a large team of policemen prepared for an incursion into the community, but before he could carry out his operation the gunmen from Tivoli Gardens peppered them with bullets and forced them to take cover and change their method. For three days there was a fierce gun battle in which 27 people were killed including members of the security forces.

Seaga ventured in the community when the fire fight almost subsided and claimed that the police had fired on the community without provocation and killed mainly women and old people. His argument was boosted by the fact that when the police had finally entered Tivoli Gardens, most of the men had already left and no weapons were recovered. The explanation given by the Police Commissioner Francis Forbes was that the men had fled the community via underground tunnels. The presence of those tunnels were never verified but there has always been lingering feelings that something is amiss in this fortified zone. It is known to the security forces and to the intelligence community that the largest cache of illegal weapons is ensconced in this bunkered area but men are usually absent when the security invades and weapons are missing as well. It is believed that Christopher Dudus Coke is the military leader of the area.

His latest publicity is a position that he does not crave. He has consistently shunned the limelight but wheels and deals in the background. Whether it is about Bruce Golding taking the parliamentary seat after Seaga was forced into retirement, or if his lawyer, Tom Tavares Finson should be ordained in the post, he was very powerful in the decision-making process if Bruce Golding became Member of Parliament for the area and ultimately Prime Minister.

With Bruce Golding beholden to him for his power and prestige, it was not surprising that when Coke's extradition to the United States was requested Bruce as Prime Minister could not separate himself from the proceedings and manufactured all kinds of reasons why the extradition was not prepared in conformity with Treaty between Jamaica and the United States. At first Golding explained that the evidence provided was illegally obtained by the US and breached the Jamaican wiretap laws. Bruce postulated that the policeman who provided the evidence to the law enforcement authorities in the United States was not authorized to do so because he did not follow the chain of command as laid down in the law and hence he was wanted by the Jamaican government to face charges, which attracted a prison sentence and a huge fine.

It was puzzling to many people who thought that Bruce Golding would have been receptive to whistle blowers. He had come to power just a couple years before championing whistleblower protection and vouched that if elected he would introduce legislation to protect such persons. In fact, he came to power because the PNP led by Portia Simpson Miller, was involved into a kickback deal with a Dutch oil company known as Trafigura, in which a government minister serving Portia was given thirty one million dollars that was used to fund the PNP's annual conference. The banking transaction was leaked to Golding by a bank official, who brought the matter to the parliament and sucked every political mileage that he could gain from it. To provide banking information in the manner in which it was received by Golding was illegal but it was of great public assistance, he thought, and he was convinced that the law had to provide a buffer for those persons. He provided a top job in his administration for 'his' whistleblower.

Bruce used the Jamaican Parliament to berate the United States in the protection of Dudus and made it appear as if the US wanted to breach the constitutional rights of a 'Jamaican' and that he was willing to pay a political price in the protection of this favored person. He was constantly questioned in the parliament by the former minister of National Security, Dr Peter Phillips about the delay in his Administration, signing the extradition order and preparing an extradition warrant as prescribed by the treaty. His stout defense elicited wide discussion among the populace about the position of Dudus Coke in his constituency and thought that it was a legitimate concern and others wanted the US to provide more evidence as demanded by Golding.

For nine months Golding vacillated on the issue and Phillips who was accused by Karl Samuda, the JLP's General Secretary of working for the CIA continued to delve deeper into Golding's refusal and brought a bombshell before the parliament. He asked Golding in a question and answer session if he knew about the engagement of the government of a US law firm from Chicago- Manatt, Phelps

& Phillips who was retained to argue the case on behalf of the government, ostensibly to advocate for Coke. Golding denied any knowledge of the government's involvement, but on the following day he gave an explanation that he had made checks and found that a lawyer from the aforementioned law firm had 'only by chance', met the Jamaican Solicitor General on a flight to Washington. It was later revealed that the lawyer from Manatt was invited to sit in on a meeting at the US State Department discussing the Coke matter but that he was not retained.

Bruce continued his obfuscation for many weeks and his post-cabinet press briefings conducted by his Information Minister was overshadowed by what became as the 'Manatt affair'. He relented, somewhat, and appointed Karl Samuda to investigate the government's involvement in the affair. Samuda seemed to have completely messed up his answers to the media and the lawyer that was retained to engage Manatt, Harold Brady, became the center of focus and he did not relish that role. He ended up blasting the Information Minister on a morning radio program and that opened a can of worms.

Bruce Golding returned from a vacation where he was involved in bird shooting and presumably returned home as a straight-shooter. He went to parliament and tried to provide answers again from Peter Phillips' questions and conceded that he had personally sanctioned the Jamaica Labour Party's involvement with the law firm to lobby the US government on the issue. He claimed that there was precedent for such engagement but did not provide and evidence to the effect. That was a bombshell and the questions from the Opposition benches were fast and furious. Golding acknowledged that when the question was first asked in parliament he distanced the government's involvement, because he had sanctioned the move as JLP leader and not as Prime Minister. He happens to occupy both positions in our system of government.

The deception that Golding portrayed caused almost the entire society, including staunch backers, to call for his resignation. The people felt betrayed because Golding had campaigned on a platform of being new and different and promised that as chief servant he would be accountable to the public and should be held to a very high standard. The public was incensed and no amount of explanation from his key allies and spokespersons could dampen the call for him to go. The people were particularly peeved because he attempted to make a distinction between his role as prime minister and party leader and they felt that the Prime Minister took them for 'idiots', and that is not something that you will get away with when dealing with Jamaicans. They felt that Bruce had lied and there was no compromise. There was massive call from home and abroad for him to demit his post. His wife went to church and the congregation prayed for her but they also held up placards for him to resign. She claimed that her husband could not say everything and the plot thickened.

Within days of his wife's revelation, that he had to be coy with certain issues, Golding appeared before the nation in a televised broadcast and apologized for his transgressions. He still gave the impression that he did not know that his party had crossed the line into government territory to achieve its objective of cutting some deal for the alleged drug trafficker and arms dealer. Many in the country accepted his apology, some people also wanted to move on, yet others still felt bitterly betrayed and wanted him to go. It was one of those Bill Clinton, Monica Lewinsky moments.

The Prime Minister promised the nation, that he would have the extradition warrant issued for Coke the following day and all hell broke loose. Dudus and his men immediately set about barricading themselves inside their fortified zone of Tivoli Gardens. Old cars, wooden structures, filled propane gas cylinders with booby traps attached and military arranged sandbags were quickly set up at strategic points ready to take on the State security forces. His cronies from all across the country came in to assist and neighboring communities were allegedly paid to disrupt the operations of the security forces as a distraction from their main focus.

About eight thousand people marched into the streets in support of their 'Robin Hood' the day after the Prime Minister's announcement that Dudus would be arrested. There were placards that suggested that they would die for him. The women declared that he was their benefactor and supported their children going to school and provided food for their tables. There were even dogs fitted with cardboard tags with markings in support of this overlord. Dudus felt emboldened and his fighters could be seen openly parading in the community with their rifles, ready for a fight.

Sunday May 23, 2010 will be remembered in Jamaica as the day that the security mobilized against criminals in their biggest numbers. The 'mother of all garrisons', Tivoli Gardens was their target. They sent out a message to the law-abiding residents of the area that they should leave the community and with the atmosphere so tense in Downtown Kingston, buses had stopped running and therefore the security forces promised the residents that buses would have been provided at strategic points. The residents even if they wanted to leave, could not do so, because the gunmen guarding Coke would have trained their guns on them.

The residents remained in their homes and it presented an ominous sign. The military and police had surrounded the community and the warning to get out did not sound empty and the history of the security forces pummeling Tivoli with their heaviest guns was not unusual. Many times previously innocent citizens have lost their lives in similar encounters. I thought that lessons were learnt and so I suspected that this time more military precision would have been applied. I don't know where I got the idea that things had changed in the mindset of the State. Maybe it was because Bruce Golding had promised that he would ensure the human rights of all its citizens and more so because he is the Member of Parliament for the area.

Monday, May 24, will be forever etched in the minds of Jamaicans and many around the world as one of the bloodiest days ever witnessed. The State security forces pulverized the community with their guns and equipment that they said was used to breach walls and which the residents described as bombs. It is reminiscent of the events in Waco, Texas. Bodies were sprawled into the middle of the community riddled with bullets and on the first day of the operation the official figure given by the government was forty four killed and four guns recovered.

The people were shocked at the number of weapons that were found. It was expected that the police would have come up with their highest ever cache of illegal weapons. The reports prior to the invasion gave the public the impression that there were possibly hundreds of men in the community armed with high-powered weapons and they would rid the society of them. Rather than the security

forces coming out as victors; questions were being asked about the success of their mission. The man most wanted was missing, hundreds of men from the community disappeared and the guns were gone. The police and military were at pains to explain it and once again they resorted to the oft-repeated claim that the men may have escaped via tunnels in the area. This was compounded by the resident's claims that they had been harassed by soldiers and police and that innocent people were killed in cold blood right before their eyes.

The residents also argued that the soldiers were burning some of the bodies. This was flatly denied, but a day later the security forces were filmed in the May Pen Cemetery, a few hundred yards from Tivoli Gardens, attempting to bury some of the bodies recovered from site of the massacre. Some of these bodies, posted on the internet, had visible burn marks and scalding skins and protruding intestines. The post-mortem results should be very interesting. The autopsies were set for a week later but when the families showed up for the appointment they were told that the independent forensic pathologist who was scheduled to participate had not arrived into the island.

Independence

Since Independence we have been hearing terms such as 'better must come', 'deliverance', 'we put people first', 'structural adjustment', 'liberalization', 'bang belly economy' and 'light at the end of the tunnel'- all good sounding terms but what do we have to show for them?

We are witnessing economic impoverishment, where about half of our population lives below the poverty line. We have a run-down civil service that sometimes treats its citizens like garbage. We have a murder rate that ranks us at the pinnacle among other nations. We have one of the highest per capita debts in the world and what do we have to show for it? Major highways from one end of the island to the other end, excellent health care for our citizens, water in every nook and cranny, a top class educational system. None of those exists and painfully so.

The fathers of our independence proclaimed that their mission was to achieve political independence and the next generation was responsible for achieving our economic independence. The big question is; did we achieve political independence? Or did we establish a system to massage the ego of our politicians? If our ability to vote for leaders who do not consult us before making decisions or account to us after deciding our fates, is considered political independence, then I think that our forefathers have failed miserably.

We cannot achieve political independence without economic independence. The United States can dictate to us but they cannot dictate to Singapore, because Singapore does not have to stretch their hands to the US for any hand-out. The economic independence of Jamaica is a long way off. Our children's future has been heavily

mortgaged and it will take a miracle to get them out of their indebtedness, (although they have not borrowed a cent).

Absolutely nothing is wrong with being independent. What is of utmost importance is that we manage our affairs well. We need to be able to prevent our leaders from selling our future earnings from Bauxite for today's consumption. We desperately need a revolution in our political structure. The present system has not worked and will not work. In 1998 Ronnie Thwaites, a Member of Parliament for the ruling party, after the financial crisis, said that we were witnessing one of the most massive transfers of resources from the poor to the rich since slavery was abolished. In that same year, Perneal Charles a Trade Unionist and someone who previously served as a government minister said that the conditions in the cane fields are worse now than they were during slavery. Something is radically wrong with this picture.

Conclusion

In re-awakening the people, this present government led by Bruce Golding will have to find a way to launch a massive assault on crime. It is clear that the people that he has appointed as National Security Ministers have no answer to the crime problem. In two years Golding appointed Derrick Smith, Colonel Trevor McMillan and now the worst of all Dwight Nelson. The crime problem is engulfing the nation and has been so, for at least the last two decades. People are cowering in fear, families are scampering home before nightfall to try and avoid the marauding gunmen.

The crime problem is a national crisis and needs to be treated as such. The entire country needs to be mobilized around the issue. If it takes three thousand policemen and soldiers to flood a crime-infested area like Spanish Town for one year or more, then so be it. They should not leave until all the guns are found and the criminals apprehended and brought to justice or bring justice to them. Too often, we go in and leave as soon as the situation is quieted.

The questions are going to be asked about the manpower and the necessary resources to handle these situations for a sustained period. Remember, it is a national emergency- therefore, everything else is secondary. Every able-bodied man and woman need to be summoned. It has to be dealt with and we need to do it now. How can the police force be short of motor vehicles when there are countless numbers of other vehicles from other ministries gallivanting around the city? If we consider this as the most important issue facing the country, then we need to rope in those resources. This is going to take prime ministerial leadership and that is what I want to see.

The dons walking around in the crime-infested

communities, acting like Robin Hoods, should be captured under a new Racketeer Influenced and Corrupt Organization Act (RICO). Rico has been effectively used in the United States to shut down the mafia. It covers extortionists, money launderers, gun traders, murderers, illegal drug sales and prostitution etc.

The effects will come to naught if we do not tackle the nastiness and downright criminal behavior in our schools. Boot camps should be immediately set up in every parish, staffed and run by the military. The students who persistently display deviant behavior should spend time in the boot camps until they learn the norms and standards that society expects. The education minister should quickly put his list of recalcitrant students who should be immediately shipped off to these camps.

The government will need to work closely with the opposition party to achieve some meaningful targets. We cannot have gunmen ambushing and killing members of the security forces. We cannot continue to have three thousand six hundred people killed in two and a half years under this government's leadership. It was not much better under the PNP's governance.

The killing of our citizens in broad daylight in the busiest parts of the city just cannot continue. The criminals act with impunity and know that it is unlikely that they will be caught. They know that only a few people have guns to defend themselves, and therefore, they have no fear. The government may need to have civilians vetted and trained in policing and possibly military tactics to deal with this life and death situation.

We must remove our young men who hang out on the streets into compulsory military service, HEART, or the National Youth Service. We could set up a civilian police force under which will fall the Port Security Corp, Transport Authority, a new Praedial Larceny Corp, Traffic Enforcement Team, Examination Depots and Customs. Many of these bodies are not working as effectively as they could and should fall under a new agency known as the Social Renewal Task Force and headed by our most active and fearless civil servant, Danville Walker. He should be assisted by Joan Gordon Webley at the National Solid Waste Management Authority. They are two very capable civil servants.

Prime Minister Golding needs to take a direct hands-on approach to this problem. He needs to personally see to the dismantling of the garrisons and zinc fences in all the inner-city communities. City Planners need to be working on a 24-hour rotation to redesign our inner-cities. Where they have to remain, we will have to build major roads through them and open up and beautify them. We will need to provide motorist who travel through them and the citizens who live there, with a nice, calm and tranquil environment.

The Tourism Product Development Company and The Tourism Enhancement Fund should provide the funding for this new agency and to make tourism in the inner-cities a major priority.

The Private Sector Organization of Jamaica (PSOJ) should not wait until another of its prominent members is killed before marching again and to say once more that they did not know that people lived in the squalid conditions that exist in some inner-city communities.

We must realize clearly that the strife and bitterness that exist in the ghettos stem from the continued hatred of years of animosity. There are many tales of whose father killed the other man's father and whose brother killed whom.

We will not be able to adequately resolve these issues until we can thrash them out at a Truth and Reconciliation Commission, where amnesty is offered so that people can speak freely. This has to be a moment of repentance and confession and bring the whole country to the table and bear all our ills. We will then let bygones be bygones and start a new powerful social order. We will equip our people with the necessities that they need to move their lives forward. We will create a real government and private citizen's partnership. The government will work at establishing a creative and effective civil service that will offer excellent customer service to the population and to end corruption in all spheres of our lives.